BFI Film Classics

The BFI Film Classics is a series of books that introduces, interprets and celebrates landmarks of world cinema. Each volume offers an argument for the film's 'classic' status, together with discussion of its production and reception history, its place within a genre or national cinema, an account of its technical and aesthetic importance, and in many cases, the author's personal response to the film.

For a full list of titles available in the series, please visit our website: <www.palgrave.com/bfi>

'Magnificently concentrated examples of flowing freeform critical poetry.'
Uncut

'A formidable body of work collectively generating some fascinating insights into the evolution of cinema.'
Times Higher Education Supplement

'The series is a landmark in film criticism.'
Quarterly Review of Film and Video

Detour

Noah Isenberg

palgrave
macmillan

A BFI book published by Palgrave Macmillan

First published in 2008 by
PALGRAVE MACMILLAN
Houndmills, Basingstoke, Hampshire RG21 6XS and
175 Fifth Avenue, New York, N.Y. 10010
Companies and Representatives throughout the world

on behalf of the

BRITISH FILM INSTITUTE
21 Stephen Street, London W1T 1LN
<www.bfi.org.uk>

There's more to discover about film and television through the BFI.
Our world-renowned archive, cinemas, festivals, films, publications and learning
resources are here to inspire you.

PALGRAVE MACMILLAN is the global academic imprint of the Palgrave Macmillan
division of St Martin's Press, LLC and of Palgrave Macmillan Ltd.
Macmillan® is a registered trademark in the United States, United Kingdom
and other countries. Palgrave is a registered trademark in the European
Union and other countries.

Series cover design: Ashley Western
Series text design: ketchup/SE14
Images from Detour, © Producers Releasing Corporation.

Set by Cambrian Typesetters, Camberley, Surrey
Printed in China

This book is printed on paper suitable for recycling and made from fully
managed and sustained forest sources. Logging, pulping and manufacturing
processes are expected to conform to the environmental regulations of the
country of origin.

British Library Cataloguing-in-Publication Data
A catalogue record for this book is available from the British Library

ISBN 978–1–84457–239–7

Contents

Acknowledgments

During the extended research that led up to and encompassed the writing of this book, I incurred a number of debts I wish to recognise. For the preliminary work on Edgar G. Ulmer, I was aided by generous grant support from the National Endowment for the Humanities, the Feuchtwanger Memorial Library, the Austrian Fulbright-Kommission and the International Research Centre for Cultural Studies in Vienna. Similarly, my research has benefited from the kind assistance of a number of individuals: Michael Pogorzelski, Barbara Hall and Kristine Krueger at the Academy of Motion Picture Arts and Sciences and the Margaret Herrick Library; Alexander Horwath, Regina Schlagnitweit and Elisabeth Streit at the Vienna Film Museum; and Gerrit Thies at the Paul Kohner Archive of the Berlin Film Museum. When it came to providing the bulk of the source material – letters, interviews, unpublished papers, reviews, publicity stills, family photos and more – no single individual offered more magnanimous support than Arianné Ulmer Cipes, the president of the Edgar G. Ulmer Preservation Corporation and daughter of the film-maker.

While working on the project, and on Ulmer more generally, I have had the good fortune of receiving invaluable feedback and material from other scholars. In that vein, I wish to thank John Belton, Gerd Gemünden, Stefan Grissemann, Michael Palm and especially Dana Polan, who critiqued, most judiciously and perceptively, several drafts of the manuscript and who offered terrific encouragement from the initial conception up to the final execution. Several of my colleagues at the New School have lent various forms of support: Linda Dunne, Robert Polito, Meghan Roe, Ann-Louise Shapiro and Jonathan Veitch. I also wish to thank the anonymous readers' reports for their constructive observations, calling attention to various rough spots and making apt suggestions for revisions. Finally, at the BFI I would like to thank Rebecca Barden for her wisdom and sage advice throughout all stages of the project's development.

Much of this book was written during an intense summer stay in La Jolla, California, where I spent my teenage years. Over the span of a couple months, I quickly became a die-hard habitué at the town's public library, appropriately located about a mile up the road from Raymond Chandler's former digs and from the killer surf of Windansea Beach, that not-so-noir locale of my youth. Fuelled on fish tacos, and on the perpetual energy transmitted from my partner in crime, Melanie Rehak, a professional writer whose editorial generosity, personal commitment and respect for the deadline have long inspired great awe in me, my writing schedule had the intermittent feel of one of Ulmer's feverish six-day shoots. It is in no small measure thanks to her, our son Jules and my extended family and friends in Southern California that this book made it out of the gate. Needless to say, any shortcomings, oversights or missed opportunities are mine alone.

1 An Unlikely Story

Every day, to earn my daily bread
I go to the market where lies are bought,
Hopefully
I take up my place among the sellers.

> Bertolt Brecht, 'Hollywood' (1942)

How could a film that was shot on a girdle-tight schedule, with no big-name talent, no real sets to speak of – just a couple of dingy motel rooms, a roadside diner, a low-rent nightclub and a Lincoln convertible flooded with an abundance of rear projection – and a legendary 'lemonade-stand budget' ultimately attain such classic status as Edgar G. Ulmer's *Detour*?[1] Sure, for standard second-billing fare, the film earned some hearty praise in the industry trade papers and the popular press when it was first released the week after Thanksgiving 1945. Even so, at the time of its debut, it would have been all but unthinkable that this unvarnished, gritty little B-picture would ever make it into the celebrated pantheon of film noir, let alone into the National Film Registry of the Library of Congress. Indeed, it wasn't for many years, decades really, that the film found its most ardent following and finally outran its fate as the bastard child of one of Hollywood's lowliest Poverty Row studios.

Humble origins

Detour began its long, twisted career as a slim 1939 pulp novel by Martin Goldsmith, an aspiring New York writer still in his mid-twenties at the time of publication, who had made Hollywood his base of operation by the late 30s. Goldsmith's only other credits were another pulp, his first, *Double Jeopardy*, which he published the previous year, and a smattering of short stories sold to such magazines as *Script* and *Cosmopolitan*. Begging comparison to James M. Cain, and crafted in the style of the grand masters (Chandler, Hammett and others), Goldsmith's *Detour* was hailed by *The New York Times*, in the hard-boiled parlance of the day, as 'a red-hot, fast-stepping little number'. While he was still in his teens, on the eve of the Great Depression, Goldsmith had set out, much like the protagonist of his novel, to journey cross-country from New York 'via the thumb-route'. Several years later, he reportedly financed the writing of *Detour* by loading people into the back of his Buick station wagon and driving them, at '$25 a head', from New York to Los Angeles.[2] In October 1944, after a long dry spell with no sign of the film rights to his book ever being purchased, Goldsmith pawned them off on producer Leon Fromkess, President and Head of Production at Producers Releasing Corporation (PRC).

One of the early cut-rate studios on Hollywood's Poverty Row, PRC was famous for churning out cheap wartime entertainment, its three-letter company abbreviation sometimes mockingly referred to as 'Pretty Rotten Crap'.[3] Together with Monogram and Republic, PRC was one of the most storied studios in the 'B-Hive'. It existed for a mere three years, from 1943 to 1946, before becoming Eagle-Lion Studios and eventually getting folded into United Artists in the early 50s. B-movies, which thrived in America throughout the 40s, were initially conceived as the bottom half of a double bill, in many cases as mere filler for a three-hour film programme that included newsreels and trailers for the price of a single admission. More generically, they were modest boilerplate features made on a severely limited budget, the kind of movies 'in which the sets shake when an actor slams the door'.[4] The agreement between Goldsmith and PRC was announced by Edwin Schallert in the *Los Angeles Times*, in an industry round-up of recent transactions, noting a supposed affinity between Goldsmith's 'murder mystery affair' and Cain's *Double Indemnity* and including a few gossipy details on the exchange: 'Price is reported as $15,000, which is good for an independent.'[5]

Studio portrait of
Tom Neal

The lead actors selected for the film were all relatively unknown
players from the American B-movie circuit. Ulmer had already
worked together with Tom Neal, 'a poor man's Clark Gable', on
Club Havana (1945), one of his fly-by-night melodramas for PRC.
With the handsome looks of an ex-boxer and a preternatural capacity
for sulking, Neal was cast in the role of sad sack Al Roberts, a
talented New York pianist who, in his desperate attempt to reach his
fiancée in Los Angeles, gets dealt a bad hand a couple of times over.
The fiancée, Sue Harvey, a nightclub singer and aspiring starlet
turned hash-slinger, is played by Claudia Drake, a platinum-blonde
with few spoken lines and precious little time on camera. In the more
critical role of Vera, Al's acid-tongued nemesis, a thoroughly down-
and-out dame who fiendishly drops into the picture midway and
keeps things in a headlock until her unceremonious exit, a feisty

Studio portrait of
Ann Savage

actress with a curiously apt *nom de guerre*, Ann Savage (née Bernice
Maxine Lyon), was cast. Savage and Neal had previously played
opposite each other in a few Bs for Columbia – William Castle's
Klondike Kate (1943), Lew Landers's *Two-Man Submarine* (1944)
and Herman Rotsten's *The Unwritten Code* (1944) – and the two
had an established screen chemistry and a bit of history, both on and
off screen. (While shooting their first film together in 1943, Neal
purportedly wasted no time overstepping the boundaries of
professionalism, making an untoward pass at Savage by burying his
tongue deep in her ear; she is said to have rewarded him with a
prompt grazing of her knuckles across his face.[6]) Savage was brought
in to see Ulmer on the set of *Club Havana*, with just over a week left
before the shooting of *Detour* began; after a quick once-over, she
immediately fell into favour with the director. Finally, Edmund
MacDonald, who plays the amiable, pill-popping Florida bookie

Charles Haskell, Jr, a man who gives Al a lift and – after revealing a few of his deepest, darkest secrets – ends up leaving him with more than just a free meal at a truck stop, was a character actor who had been around the block a few times, earning minor roles at PRC (one with Claudia Drake), Columbia, Paramount and elsewhere.

After Goldsmith and Fromkess settled the deal, a rumour circulated that actor John Garfield, who would soon go on to play an updated Al Roberts character in Tay Garnett's *The Postman Always Rings Twice* (1946), had read the novel and was eager to have Warner Bros. acquire the rights for him (Ann Sheridan was thought of for the role of Sue and Ida Lupino for Vera). The A-league studio reportedly made an offer to Fromkess of $25,000, but Fromkess, sensing he had his hands on a good pick, was unwilling to part with the material; subsequent talk of having Garfield come to PRC on loan-out from Warners never amounted to anything.[7] In a serious break with Hollywood convention, Fromkess hired Goldsmith to write the screenplay from his own novel.[8] What he produced was an elaborate, meandering text that would have required shooting a film with a run time of some two and half hours: indeed, more than twice the length of the sixty-eight minutes to which the film would finally be restricted. With seasoned input from associate producer/writer Martin Mooney, who had many PRC productions under his belt, and from Ulmer himself – who would later take much of the credit and rather emphatically dismiss Goldsmith's novel as 'a very bad book' – the script was pared down to a manageable length. Entire sections had to be tossed out, others radically revised, and yet the threadbare quality it finally acquired, despite its intermittent reliance on the total suspension of disbelief, made for a good match with Ulmer's minimalist, rough-hewn aesthetic.

In a considerable departure from Goldsmith's novel, the tale is told exclusively from Al Roberts's perspective. Roberts serves as the film's narrator – delivering half his lines in a pained, edgy voice-over – whose primary task, beyond recounting his life as a cursed nightclub pianist and a cursed hitchhiker, is explaining the inexplicable, proving to himself, as well as to the audience, that he is essentially powerless in his losing battle against fate. The story of Al Roberts begins where it ends: on the open highway. Seated at the counter of a Nevada diner, in a tableau that evokes the canvas of Edward Hopper's iconic 1942 painting *Nighthawks*, Roberts cries into his coffee mug. The tale he tells, whittled down from Goldsmith's oversized script, is one of loss, with a tragic core that intensifies as the human wreckage piles up all around him until he is no longer able to find a way out. Al and Sue were once happily in love; they were, in Al's words, 'an ordinary healthy romance', and he was a 'pretty lucky guy' (the film's theme song 'I Can't Believe that You're in Love with Me', which plays a vital role in triggering Al's flashbacks, was *their* song). But all this changes when Sue decides to try her luck in Hollywood – a fateful decision tantamount to jilting Al at the altar – sending things into a tailspin. Sue's sudden absence cripples Al, shatters his dreams, and breeds resentment and bitterness. Yet when the opportunity arises to reunite with Sue in Los Angeles, he leaps at it, heading off on a cross-country journey with the initial giddiness of a young boy on Christmas morning.

The journey, a white-knuckle ride down a mercilessly bleak desert highway, quickly turns sour. Al becomes entangled in an impermeable web of lies and deception, starting with the panicked swapping of his identity for Haskell's, after Haskell's mysterious death leaves him in a fix, and ending with Vera's schemes of blackmail and extortion. By the film's denouement, Al finds himself completely unhinged, with blood on his hands.

Ulmer's breakthrough

Edgar Ulmer came to *Detour* at the apex of his four-year, eleven-film stint at PRC. An uncompromising Viennese aesthete, he had begun his training in Europe with Max Reinhardt, first venturing to the United States from Vienna in 1924, when Reinhardt's play *The Miracle* was enjoying a successful run at New York's Century Theatre. He went on to Hollywood to work in Universal's art

Self-portrait of
Edgar G. Ulmer

department and to assist F. W. Murnau, earning a credit as assistant art director on Murnau's first American film, *Sunrise* (1927). He then returned to Europe to work on a couple of obscure, independent pictures – as production assistant on Louis Ralph's adventure film *Flucht in die Fremdenlegion* (*Escape to the Foreign Legion*, 1929) and as a set builder on Robert Land's *Spiel um den Mann* (*Play around a Man*, 1929) – and to pick up a credit as co-director of the acclaimed late Weimar silent *Menschen am Sonntag* (*People on Sunday*, 1930), filmed in Berlin in 1929 and created by a distinguished crew of budding Hollywood transplants (Robert and Curt Siodmak, Billy Wilder, Fred Zinnemann and Eugen Schüfftan).

Ulmer ended up at PRC many years after what had turned out to be a miserable false start as a Hollywood studio director at Universal, where in 1934 he made his debut with the visually ambitious but professionally damaging horror film *The Black Cat*. (After defying studio boss Carl Laemmle in more ways than one – sneaking in a highbrow classical score to enhance the extravagant visual flourishes of the film, and stealing away the wife of Laemmle's dear nephew Max Alexander while working on the set – he was branded *persona non grata* at Universal and beyond.) During the 30s, he bounced around, directing a string of pictures outside the studio system and far from Hollywood in nearly every respect: a low-budget Western, *Thunder over Texas* (1934), released under a pseudonym; a Canadian quota quickie *From Nine to Nine* (1936); a number of health shorts aimed at ethnic audiences; and finally, working in and around New York City throughout the late 30s, he directed a pair of Ukrainian operettas, four well-received Yiddish features and the all-black musical drama *Moon over Harlem* (1939). At PRC, he took on a mix of simple, wartime potboilers (which included such titles, all from 1943, as *My Son the Hero*, *Girls in Chains* and *Jive Junction*) and a few films that pushed the generic boundaries and brought him back to his European roots (*Bluebeard*, his Faust-inspired horror film indebted to a Weimar-era aesthetic, released in 1944, and one of his final films for PRC, *Her Sister's Secret*, a 1946 weepie *à la* Douglas Sirk, among others). *Detour*, however, distinguished itself from the

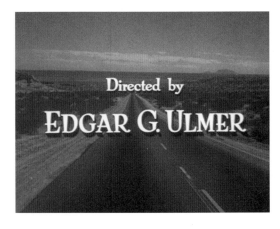

Ulmer's director credit

rest, not only in its comparatively generous reception and its unanticipated staying power, but also in its personal connection to the director and his identification with the project.

La politique des auteurs

Following a path similarly circuitous to the career of its director, *Detour* was first rediscovered in the mid-50s, hard on the heels of several unexpected paeans to Ulmer by French critics in the pages of *Cahiers du cinéma* – the same unwavering auteurists who took special delight in finding virtues in the depraved, neglected and misunderstood renegade directors (e.g. Anthony Mann, Fritz Lang, Nicholas Ray) toiling on the fringes of Hollywood. In 1956, Luc Moullet famously dubbed Ulmer 'le plus maudit des cinéastes', and though he may not be the *most* 'accursed' of film-makers – that same year François Truffaut referred to his work as 'a small gift from Hollywood', and rated Ulmer among his most beloved – his career, and even the reception of what is arguably his most famous film, often appeared utterly doomed. Like the *poète maudit* on which the term is based, the *cinéaste maudit* has been commonly understood as a romantic, tragic figure, whose style and sensibility spurn the dominant norms, who is self-consciously outré or oppositional. The French critics at *Cahiers du cinéma* gravitated toward this idea with uncommon zeal; to label a director or a film 'maudit' was to accord special status (Fritz Lang's *M*, 1931, was released in France under the title *M le maudit*), to recognise an aesthetic whose greatness was, perhaps, accepted by a mere few, but by those who were the true purveyors of the cultural avant-garde.[9]

With a bit of lag time, allowing for the methods and modes to make their way across the Atlantic, the American auteur critics took their cue from the French. Writing in his immensely influential history of American film of 1968, Andrew Sarris detected in Ulmer 'the signature of a genuine artist' and went on to hail *Detour* as 'a poetic conceit from Poverty Row'.[10] In the early 70s, Peter Bogdanovich's extensive interview with the director, first published in *Film Culture*, together with Myron Meisel's pioneering essay 'The Primacy of the

Visual' and John Belton's early composite study *Howard Hawks, Frank Borzage, Edgar G. Ulmer* (1974), helped confer upon Ulmer – and upon his finest work – the stamp of legitimacy. For Meisel, '*Detour* follows the route of mad poetic tragedy', and harbours stylistic affinities with F. W. Murnau's *Tabu* (1931); here Meisel reiterated Sarris's pronouncement of Ulmer as the true 'executor of the Murnau estate', someone who remained 'faithful to his trust'. Belton, for his part, argued that 'the bleakness of *Detour* qualifies it for pre-eminence in the cinema of fear, paranoia and insanity, alongside such classics as Samuel Fuller's *Shock Corridor* (1963), Andre de Toth's *Day of the Outlaw* (1959) and Nicholas Ray's *Bigger than Life* (1956)'.[11]

But despite such accolades, and such unmistakably flattering comparisons, throughout much of the 70s and a good part of the 80s *Detour* remained largely a private treasure among the interested few. It became what the Germans like to call a *Geheimtipp*, a favourite among those in the know, like film buffs and cult fans, a film that aired occasionally on late-night television, circulated in the hands of collectors in grainy 16mm prints, but otherwise remained essentially consigned to oblivion. If one searched hard enough, one could find a stray review or reconsideration of the film in small-circulation, minor American outlets like *Movietone News*, a magazine of the Seattle Film Society, and in the underground newspapers or fanzines like *Filmfax*. In Britain, where the film was even less accessible, a couple of brief reviews appeared in *Films and Filming* and the *Monthly Film Bulletin* in the early 80s, and a more extensive scholarly analysis, one of the first of its kind, was published by Tania Modleski in *Screen* in 1982.

King of the Bs

A watershed moment in the afterlife of *Detour* occurred when, in October 1983, UCLA's Melnitz Theatre hosted a two-month retrospective of Ulmer, declaring him the 'King of the Bs'. As the inaugural event of the retrospective, a screening of *Detour* was announced in the arts section of the *Los Angeles Times*, which saw fit to eulogise the picture as 'one of the most relentlessly intense psychological thrillers anyone has ever filmed'.[12] Ulmer had died of a stroke over a decade earlier and his lead man Tom Neal – to whom fate was equally unkind off screen – passed away just months before him. But Ann Savage, who had long been off the Hollywood radar screen and was working at the time in a Los Angeles law office, found her way to the screening that night. When the house lights went on, Shirley Ulmer, Edgar's widow, script supervisor and lifelong collaborator, took to the stage to field questions. When someone enquired about the status of the actress who played Vera, Shirley responded, 'No one knows what became of Ann Savage.' At that moment, Savage found the courage in herself, plenty of which she had mustered up in her ground-breaking performance some forty years earlier, to announce 'I'm here'. She was soon the subject of a lengthy profile in the *Los Angeles Times*, 'So Whatever Happened to Bad Girl Ann Savage?', and her film career, which included over thirty pictures in total, received a new wave of recognition.[13]

Together with its principal actress, *Detour* resurfaced and made its presence known in unexpected corners. The 'King of the Bs' retrospective travelled on, under the auspices of the German cultural and educational forum, the Goethe-Institute, to less film-saturated American cities like Houston and Atlanta, where it was greeted with considerable praise and a touch of bafflement. The *Houston Chronicle* ran an article entitled 'Edgar G. Who?' in which the author, invoking America's oft-forgotten thirteenth president, declared Ulmer 'the Millard Fillmore of film directors', who is 'at last getting respect'. The same author then went on to summarise *Detour* as 'an hour-long gripe and bicker session between a guilty drifter and a hitchhiker, set in the 5 o'clock shadow of 40's fatalism', giving the film one of its catchiest one-line tags.[14] In a piece published in the *Atlanta Constitution*, the author recounts an interview with Shirley Ulmer, who remarked of her husband's talent as a director of minor independent films: 'Today, they're called art pictures. That's the switch. He had to use these artistic means to cover up a small budget. He had to have lots of imagination.'[15]

In the case of *Detour*, that sort of resourceful imagination seems finally to have paid off. When *Time* magazine ran a 1987 cover story, 'The Thriller is Back', on Adrian Lyne's *Fatal Attraction*, it singled out *Detour*, including a tempestuous production still of Ann Savage and Tom Neal, as one of the film's critical antecedents. Earlier that same year, the American Film Institute's magazine *American Film* published an article, 'On the Road: Ten Films that Put You in the Driver's Seat', which placed *Detour* in the good company of Raoul Walsh's *They Drive by Night* (1940), Arthur Penn's *Bonnie and Clyde* (1967) and Dennis Hopper's *Easy Rider* (1969). It was not long before video recordings, generally of poor quality, were in wide circulation, and a mass audience finally gained access to the film.

Indeed, by the 90s, *Detour* was no longer merely the darling of the subterranean cultists, nor the exclusive subject of rarefied academic conversation, but had begun to enter the mainstream. In 1992, it was declared worthy of inclusion in the National Film Registry at the Library of Congress, the only B-picture to have earned the honour. Not long after, it was featured in large-scale Ulmer retrospectives in New York and Edinburgh, and was released on DVD, first individually and then in a variety of film noir box sets. In 1998, *Premiere* magazine ranked *Detour* among the '100 Movies that Shook the World', and that same year, the *Chicago Sun-Times* film critic Roger Ebert, famous for his generally banal weekly television reviews, took it upon himself to speculate about the hidden merits and remarkably odd career of this pock-marked little picture:

Detour is a movie so filled with imperfections that it would not earn the director a passing grade in film school. This movie from Hollywood's poverty row, shot in six days, filled with technical errors and ham-handed narrative, starring a man who can only pout and a woman who can only sneer, should have faded from sight soon after it was released in 1945. And yet it lives on, haunting and creepy, an embodiment of the guilty soul of *film noir*. No one who has seen it has easily forgotten it.[16]

Regardless of what one may think of Ebert's 'thumbs-up/thumbs-down' school of film reviewing, he manages to get to the heart of some of *Detour*'s most enduring qualities: its tendency to get inside the viewer's head – analogous, perhaps, to the viewer's inevitable engulfment by Al's panic-stricken trains of thought – and, of course, its peculiar unforgettability. Today, *Detour* is a film so iconic that a choice line from it ('Whichever way you turn, fate sticks out its foot to trip you up') can be construed, so Martin Scorsese suggests in his 1995 documentary account of American film, as a shorthand definition of the entire mood of film noir. Or, in the words of Kent Jones, '*Detour* has, at this point, become more than a film – it is now a classic of the authentically down and out, the ultimate corrective to Hollywood gloss.'[17]

2 Pulp Fictions

From the moment that the opening credits roll across the screen, we find ourselves tearing along the open road. The reverse tracking shot of a desert highway, captured from the back window of a moving car, combined with the dramatic orchestral score by Leo Erdody (a frequent collaborator during Ulmer's PRC years), immediately sets the feverish pace and the tenor of the film. We observe a single automobile, seemingly broken down on the side of road, and nothing else but barren highway before the screen fades to black and then opens up once more on a lone figure whose silhouette can barely be made out against the inky night; the only source of illumination are the headlights of a passing car. As the figure gradually fills out the frame, traipsing along in a near-somnambular state, head tilted slightly askance and hands buried in both pockets, a quick glimpse of his unshaven face betrays a deeply distraught condition. A few paces further and the frame dissolves to a two-shot of the same figure seated, his facial expression unchanged, beside the driver of a

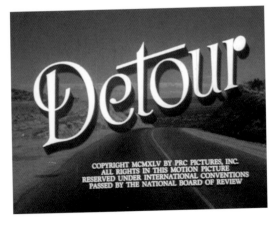

The title credit on the open highway

convertible. A pithy, rather trivial exchange of words – 'Well, here we are, I turn down here at the next block' and 'Thanks, mister, I'll get off there' – coupled with an array of flickering neon signs ('Smokes', 'News', 'Bar', 'Coffee Shop' and, finally, 'Reno: The Biggest Little City in the World') punctuate this atmosphere-drenched visual prologue, one that is nowhere to be found in Goldsmith's original screenplay, nor in his eponymous novel.

The credit sequence functions as a framing device of sorts, a means of establishing a few of the film's critical plot lines and of evoking some of the overarching themes: the lone wanderer ambles about without a clear destination on a journey that places him completely at the mercy of others, subject to chance and the contingencies of modern life; the open road, while benign and even liberating in most of American mythology, bears a distinctly gloomy quality here; the convertible sedan, a mere prop in this scene, will become one of the many confining spaces that trap the film's hero; and, in terms of the film's visual and narrative symmetry, the mood that is conveyed here will be rearticulated and further amplified in the epilogue, a scene that recasts the lone figure on a dark, desolate highway, only to be picked up one last time, a final bookend to the protracted flashbacks and voice-over narration that constitute the body of the film.

Hollywood elegies

Here, then, is where the many changes to Goldsmith's novel begin to hatch.[18] First, there are the very basic ones: violin prodigy Alexander Roth – who wastes his prodigious talent, rejecting his years of classical training, by choosing to play in a small-time jazz band – becomes piano virtuoso Al Roberts, who similarly squanders his talent at the Break O'Dawn Club. En route to Sue, Roth ends up serving time ('thrown in the jug for swiping some fruit off a stand') in Dallas, an aspect of his ill-fated journey that rates brief mention in the screenplay (where the charge is 'vagrancy'), but is never reflected on screen. More substantially, the film dispenses entirely with Sue's subjective narration – over the course of the novel's seven crisp chapters, Goldsmith alternates first-person accounts by Alex and Sue – and in doing so, cuts out several ancillary figures who are critical to Sue's more fully developed, more hard-edged character. In Goldsmith's 'Extraordinary Tale' (as the subtitle of his novel has it), not long after her arrival in Los Angeles, Sue gets involved with a slick bit player called Raoul Kildare, a man with a fake 'Hollywood-British accent' and an 'installment plan Cadillac'. They engage in what Sue nonchalantly refers to as 'straightforward sex', which is, as she tells us, 'brought about by a quantity of inferior rye which he had fed me as rapidly as I could down it'. The audacious Kildare stands in marked contrast to the soft, sensitive, ultimately pathetic Roth. After learning of Roth's supposed death (in a plot twist that remains undeveloped in the film, where we merely witness Al trading his clothes for Haskell's and, much later, hear from Al that Haskell's body is taken for his own), Sue entertains the fantasy of marrying Kildare and returning to New York, before she learns, in a deal-breaking turn of events, that he is married to one of her co-workers at the hash house.

While Ulmer, in his interview with Bogdanovich, attests to his specific attachment to the character of Al Roberts ('I was always in love with the idea, and with the main character – a boy who plays piano in Greenwich Village and really wants to be a decent pianist'), Sue's pointed commentary on Hollywood, embedded in the novel but kept from both the final screenplay and the film, would seem to speak equally well for the director. Relatively late in the extended saga, after Sue gets the official news of Roth's presumed death on his doomed highway journey, she admits to an unusually blasé attitude that has taken hold, making it possible for her to harbour a strange sense of cold detachment:

Hollywood is a peculiar spot. Once you're here, everything and everyone outside seems to be at the other end of the world. Live in Hollywood for a short while and then try to go home! You'll never be contented again. A week here will find you infected with that curious unrest that is so much a part of everyone in the colony.

Like Sue, Ulmer himself became 'infected' and in due course equally alienated by that same world. In a brief essay he wrote in the 50s, 'The Director's Responsibility', Ulmer asserts, 'To the visitor from Mars (with permission by Orson Welles), this fascinating place between the desert and the Pacific Ocean, which the world affectionately calls Hollywood, may seem, indeed, at the present time a sad and confused place.'[19]

    In Goldsmith's novel, Sue admits, despite her growing pessimism, to having big dreams – the fantasy of effecting a total makeover and changing her name to Suzanne Harmony – and to having the 'usual Hollywood hopes: a contract, some money, stardom and that sort of thing'. Sue's dreams are partly, only teasingly, fulfilled in the novel, when she gets a late call from her agent Fleishmeyer, who tells her he has arranged a screen test with David O. Selznick. Yet, in the end, the representation of Hollywood in Goldsmith's text, as in Ulmer's film, takes on a decidedly unflattering air. Sue goes on to comment, in the penultimate chapter of the novel: 'Hollywood was more sickening than ever. The studios were still impregnable fortresses, so near and yet so far beyond reach.' Not unlike the bitter pronouncements of Bertolt Brecht, whose cycle of Hollywood poems casts a harsh light on the dream factories and their shameless propensity for peddling lies, Sue's commentary is tinged with disillusionment. Alexander Roth, who in passing thinks that in Los Angeles he, too, might 'ace [himself] into pictures', makes similarly dark observations once he is driving with Vera along Hollywood Boulevard:

Down the Boulevard a neon sign kept spelling: ALL ROADS LEAD TO HOLLYWOOD – AND THE PAUSE THAT REFRESHES – DRINK COCA COLA. What a joke. That sign should have read: ALL ROADS LEAD TO HOLLYWOOD – AND THE COUNTY JAIL – DRINK POISON.

Elsewhere Goldsmith's novel may bear comparison to Cain, Chandler and Hammett, but here, with the heavy dose of Hollywood cynicism, the more apt comparisons are to Nathanael West (*The Day of the Locust*, 1939) and, with prescient anticipation, to Budd Schulberg (*What Makes Sammy Run*, 1941).

Finally, in the transition from novel to screenplay and to what ultimately made the cut in the film, all traces of Jewishness, rather profuse in Goldsmith's original story, are stripped. Gone with the chopping of Sue's story are Manny Fleishmeyer, her shady agent, and the heavily accented Mr Bloomberg, her boss at the hash house where she works. Gone, too, are Roth's Old Testament references and his sardonic questioning of whether things look 'kosher'. In the novel, we are made privy to the otherwise useless information that Alexander Roth was born Aaron Rothenberg, that he changed his name at the suggestion of his violin instructor (i.e. for professional advancement), and that when he loses all ties to his identity, after Haskell's body is found and it is taken for his own, he considers the idea that, if he is ever able to marry Sue, he will take on an alias, perhaps 'Israel Masseltof'. As Robert Polito has noted, 'Goldsmith injected such a consistent Jewish ambience into the novel that it's tempting to read the Alex–Sue saga as an ethnic allegory about Jews in America.'[20] Fully in keeping with the ways of the time, when assimilation, name-changing and affecting the dominant norms of Christian America were the order of the day, the overtly Jewish strains of Goldsmith's novel would presumably not have been considered palatable to a large filmgoing audience. The year 1945, with the horrors of the Second World War still fresh at the time of the film's release, was not an especially hospitable moment for 'an ethnic allegory about Jews in America' to hit the screen.

That's the stuff

Though Ulmer has often received credit for *Detour* as a whole, its snappy, hard-boiled dialogue, boasting words that have the power to 'crack like a whip', remains in large measure the sole achievement of

Goldsmith's screenplay, much of it extracted directly from his novel. Leading into the initial encounter between Roberts and Haskell, Goldsmith has Roberts spout a few ominous lines of voice-over ('You never know what's in store for you when you hear the squeal of brakes. If only I had known what I was getting into *that* day in Arizona . . .'). Riding in the Lincoln convertible, with the same rear projection used throughout the film and the same distraught expression that he wore in the Nevada diner, before any actual

Al and Haskell on the road

Al eyes Haskell's scar

dialogue unfolds, Al continues to offer more of his neurotic voice-over, this time with an assertion that will have wider implications for his moral compass ('You know, Emily Post ought to write a book of rules for guys thumbing rides – because, as it is now, you never know what's right and what's wrong'). Al's thoughts ultimately become transparent to Haskell, who catches him staring at the wounds on his right hand, to which the audience is directed via subjective camera.

HASKELL   Beauties, aren't they? They're gonna be scars some day. (*Pause*) What an animal!

ROBERTS   Whatever it was, it must have been pretty big and vicious to have done that.

HASKELL   Right on both counts, New York. I was tussling with the most dangerous animal in the world – a woman.

ROBERTS   She must have been Tarzan's mate. It looks like you lost the bout.

HASKELL   It certainly wasn't a draw. You know, there ought to be a law against dames with claws . . .

ROBERTS   Yeah.

HASKELL   I tossed her out of the car on her ear. (*Pause*) Was I wrong? Give a lift to a tomato, you expect her to be—nice, don't you?

ROBERTS   Yeah.

HASKELL   After all, what kind of dames thumb rides? Sunday school teachers?

ROBERTS   Yeah.

HASKELL   The little witch! She must have thought she was riding with some fall guy. And me who's been booking horses around racetracks since I was twenty. I've known a million dames like her. Two million.

ROBERTS   Yeah.

HASKELL   I stopped the car, opened the door. 'Take it on the Arthur Duffy, sister,' I told her.

ROBERTS   That's the stuff.

This particular exchange, adapted nearly verbatim from Goldsmith's novel, bears all the hallmarks of a classic pulp: the taut, muscular prose style, the clipped sentences and the requisite, almost reflexive suspicion, even contempt, of women. As the dialogue unfolds, Al becomes Haskell's yes-man, reaffirming and legitimising the choices that Haskell makes, and all of this mirroring – in equally dubious ways – the choices that Al himself will make. (In the novel, Roth fights off a moralistic commentary: 'I felt like saying that was what he got for playing around. However, I had sense enough to keep my mouth shut. What business was it of mine if he tried to manhandle some dame?') Furthermore, well before we ever meet Vera and are treated to the opportunity of a repeat performance with Al in Haskell's garb, we already possess the vague contours of the scenario told from Haskell's perspective: A female hitchhiker is picked up with the hope that she will be, no doubt sexually speaking, '*nice*'. When she rebuffs Haskell's advances, using her claws in the process, he throws her out 'on her ear', using an old O. Henry line ('Take it on the Arthur Duffy') to give a little extra force, and American folksiness, to his action.

Al's last line in the dialogue, uttered just before Haskell proceeds to tell the story of his other scar (a duelling wound), echoes the same phrase of encouragement he uses in his one-way phone conversation with Sue before embarking on his cross-country journey. He tells her 'That's the stuff,' right after announcing his intention to get married immediately upon their planned reunion in Los Angeles. As a kind of surrogate for his relationship with Sue, the ritualistic male bonding that takes place in the car serves as a foundation for their lasting association, an association from which it will in due course prove hard to shake free. By confiding in Al about his scuffle with the ferocious female hitchhiker and his failed childhood duel using his father's Franco-Prussian sabres – an event so disturbing that it prompted Haskell to run away from home, never to return again – and, more crucially, by showing Al the scars from both of these formative encounters, Haskell draws Al into a sphere of

Al and Haskell connected at
the hip

Al shadows Haskell at the
roadside diner

Al takes his turn at the wheel

intimacy that continues to deepen until Haskell's death. Haskell
insists on treating Al (whose initial gesture of wishing to wait outside
while Haskell eats alone is flagged in Goldsmith's screenplay with the
stage cue of 'phoney reluctance') to a hot meal at a roadside diner,
escorting him in to the restaurant with their arms locked, their
relationship fully consummated. He continues to tell Al more about
his past – small details of his identity, of his life story, that will
become important when Al, faced with Haskell's accidental death,
resumes the journey as Charles Haskell, Jr. When the two stand up to
pay the bill, Al shadows Haskell, their movements in perfect unison,
as if rehearsing for the role he will soon need to play. (In Goldsmith's
novel, the resemblance between Haskell and Roth is given additional
emphasis: their height and build are approximately the same, while
Roth observes of Haskell's nose, 'It was almost the duplicate of my
own.') When they are finally shown back on the road, Al is at the
wheel, where Haskell had last been, and where Al will remain for the
rest of his odyssey, most of it under the false identity of Haskell.[21]

A bundle of hate

'If there is any worse spot than for a man to find himself slave to a
woman's whims,' Roth proclaims in Goldsmith's novel, 'I'd like to
know about it.' Like Al Roberts in the film, Roth finds himself
ensnared by Vera, forever caught in her web after making the fatal
error of picking her up on the desert highway. Yet, the interaction
between Roth and Vera is slightly more revealing, more illicit and
more self-aware in the novel than in the film. Roth is, so he wants us
to believe, no dummy; he knows that female hitchhikers are 'not
exactly debutantes from The Four Hundred', nor are they the
'Sunday school teachers' of Haskell's mordant formulation. But he
takes the risk anyway, which, though seemingly inexplicable in both
film and novel, may be driven by the same ulterior motive that led
Haskell to give Vera a ride in the first place. As Roth gets a closer
look at her, after she drifts off to sleep – striking the same ominous,
deathly pose that Haskell struck just moments before her – she is

Haskell out cold

Vera as Haskell's double

suddenly viewed in a more lascivious light than in his initial
estimation (in possession of 'a beauty that is almost homely, because
it's so damned real'). In the novel, we have this: 'Her nose was nice,
turned up just a wee bit at the end; her lashes long and black and
genuine; and her breasts were small and high, the way I like breasts.'
To be sure, the protagonist's sexual appetite is more pronounced in
Goldsmith's novel, where he shows a kind of bravado entirely
missing in the film (at times, it's almost as if he's channelling the spirit
of his macho alter-ego Haskell and his inimitable come-on lines such
as, when he brashly flirts with the waitress at the diner, 'I'll be
waiting outside for you when you finish work'). It doesn't take much
to get Roth aroused, as he fleetingly considers the thought of bedding
the woman who rents him a room at his initial stopover at a roadside
motel. He has trouble, in general, keeping sex off his mind.

Roth ultimately succumbs to temptation: first, with the
misguided pick-up; then, much later, when he and Vera are holed up
in their dirty rented room in Los Angeles. In the novel, the build-up
to that particular scene bears similarities to Ulmer's adaptation, but
then Goldsmith takes liberties that a film of 1945 could not, allowing
the sexual tension between Vera and Roth to follow its logical path
toward a tryst of sorts. After bickering incessantly and tossing back
liquor in between, Vera and Roth reach an impasse; she explains that
he doesn't have to sleep on the couch anymore if he doesn't want to.

Roth tries in vain to assert his moral integrity and self-restraint ('there was one thing she couldn't make me do') before he finds himself dreaming of Sue, in an erotic vision that is essentially a sexed-up fusion of both Sue and Vera: 'an amber body writhing in the dimness, beautiful and frightening at the same time, the personification of Venus, of Bacchus, of unutterable fleshly delights'. He quickly caves in, confessing angrily to his indiscretion, 'I wanted Sue so much that night, I went into the bedroom and had Vera. There's reality for you. Go out and roll in it.'

In Ulmer's film, Vera emerges as a distillation of Goldsmith's original portrayal. She retains her essence, as it is presented in the novel, but in the written text there is more backstory that presumably could not be worked into the script, or parts of which could not have been depicted on screen:

If a person could believe her, here was a dame who'd touched bottom, who'd been batted around for five or six years from one job to another until she was groggy. She'd been a movie usher in Pittsburgh, a shoe-worker in Binghamton, a cashier in Trenton and God knows what else. She'd washed dishes, scrubbed floors, picked pockets, rolled cigars; she'd lived with cops, clerks, floor-walkers and every brand of visiting Elk imaginable. Also, she'd kept Haskell's bed warm from Shreveport to El Paso. She'd reached the stage where she hated men and when I say hated, I mean *hated* – almost as much as she hated women. That little girl was just a bundle of hate.

In Goldsmith's terse, pulp formulation: 'Vera was like a frozen stick of dynamite; you never knew when she was going to blow.' It was left to Ulmer and his crew – and, of course, up to Ann Savage's performance – to render such a singularly odious femme fatale cinematically viable.

Murder he wrote
Of the many scenes that potentially confound viewers, the depictions of the two deaths – murders, perhaps, accidents, well

maybe – are especially hard to pin down. The reworking of the story, in the transition from novel to screenplay and from screenplay to film, meant that certain fragments contained in Goldsmith's original could not be included in Ulmer's adaptation. In the film, Al is so concerned about preserving his free ride to Los Angeles, lest he be forced prematurely to say 'goodbye ticket to Hollywood', that the thought of orchestrating Haskell's murder in a premeditated sense seems anathema to him. In the novel, however, where Roth's moral character has a few more shades of grey, Goldsmith offers this:

I would be handing you a lot of Abe Lincoln baloney if I said I wasn't tempted once or twice during the night to slug Mr Haskell over the head and roll him for his cash. So I won't say it. The guy was treating me right and I couldn't bring myself to the point of hurting him. It took plenty of self-control though. Remember, I was desperately in need of money; and in the glove-compartment of the car was a small Stillson wrench and a pair of heavy driving-gloves I could have used for padding. It was a cinch set-up if there ever was one.

Knowing that the thought of 'kissing him with a wrench', as Ann Savage's Vera will later accuse Al Roberts of doing, crosses Roth's mind makes his declarations of complete innocence all the less plausible. Yet, in both cases, novel and film, part of what clouds the circumstances surrounding Haskell's death is the unmistakable poor health in which we find him. In the film, we witness him popping pills like they're gum drops, possibly to combat infection from his wounds or possibly to medicate another, more serious ailment. In Goldsmith's novel, in lieu of pills, Haskell smokes marijuana, 'reefers, sticks of jive' (in Roth's words, 'The bastard must be high as a kite on that weed'). Roth, who inadvertently smokes some of Haskell's dope when he helps himself to what he thinks is a cigarette in the car's glove compartment, becomes ill, vomiting on the side of the road in the rain; he does this before he is finally able to put up the top to the

Haskell popping his
pills like gum drops

convertible, which, as in the film rendition, requires the opening of
the passenger door and the resulting freefall of Haskell's corpse.

The death of Haskell signals, in both novel and film, a turning
point in the narrative 'where all the mess begins', as Roth tells us.
'You'll probably take the rest of the story with a grain of salt,' he
continues, 'or maybe just come right out and call me seven brands of
liar. It sounds fishy – but I can't help that, any more than I could have
helped what happened.' As with Al Roberts, it doesn't much matter
what Roth says, since we see what he ends up doing ('I'd done just
what the police would say I did even if I didn't'). After Al crosses the
California state line, he pulls into a roadside motel to try to sleep off
the trauma. Goldsmith's characterisation of Roth at this same
juncture in the story is comparatively unburdened by Haskell's death:
'I slept like a top for almost eighteen hours, and as far as I know, I
was too busy sleeping to dream about a thing.' In Ulmer's rendition,
Haskell's death is followed by a brief but poignant dream sequence
that is strikingly different from the stylised fantasy of a glittering Sue
in the limelight in which Al indulges himself while driving. Ulmer has
Al mumbling in his sleep, begging Haskell not to die for fear that he
will inevitably be held responsible. We review the scattered scenes
surrounding Haskell's death, as Al's mind seemingly becomes

Al's dream sequence
and the layering of his
tormented memories

imprisoned by his own memories. Sue is nowhere in the picture, and
the tightly framed shot of Al, clad in pyjamas (conspicuously striped
in a fashion that is suggestive of those worn by a jailbird) with his
head on the pillow, is superimposed over a chain of evocative images
that bear down on him. The sequence ends with a final
superimposition of Al's anguished face, taken from the scene of the
crime, haunting the restless figure.

With Vera's death, the contrast between novel and film is even
more extreme. In Goldsmith's original, it is a cold, matter-of-fact
account: 'She went to the phone, began calling the police and I
strangled her to death.' End of story. Well, then there's the add-on,
maybe an afterthought, underscored for emphasis: '*Accidentally,
though.*' Roth hears Vera ask for the number of the Hollywood
police station – an irony that is considerably greater in the film – and
tries in vain to pull the receiver from her. In the process, just like that,
'her throat got in the way'. By contrast, Ulmer's version, inspired in
part by the script but choreographed on the fly, is much more
dramatic. Vera runs into the bedroom with the phone cord snaked
around her neck and throws herself onto the bed in a drunken fit,
only to have Al, locked outside, yank the cord with all his might, as if
to reel her in, and in the process steal the last gasp from her lungs.

Ulmer then follows this with one of the most simple, but potent sequences in the film – Al kicks down the door and surveys the crime scene, as the subjective camera catches each and every piece of evidence (Vera's lifeless face, the telephone, her perfume and hairbrush, a bottle of whisky, her shoes, an empty garment box, her clothes and finally the phone jack), fading in and out of focus. All at once, in a state of shock, Al realises what he has just done and the impossibility of rolling back the clocks. 'This time I was guilty – knew it, felt it.'

3 Movies on the Cheap

During his four-year stint at PRC, Ulmer quickly earned a reputation
for producing consistently solid entertainment without the aid of a
big-studio budget. His output during those years was nothing short
of staggering. He directed three feature-length films in 1945, four in
1943 and several others in between, making him, together with Sam
Newfield, PRC's most prolific and most sought-after director.
'Nobody had ever made good pictures faster and for less money than
Edgar Ulmer,' maintains Peter Bogdanovich.[22] With his uncanny
knack for squeezing in an impossibly high number of set-ups – as
many as eighty – per day, and in most cases shooting everything he
needed in under a week, he was, at least in this respect, capable of
putting a smile on the faces of the men in the front office. As Ulmer
would explain to Bogdanovich, he liked to think of himself at the
time as the 'Capra of PRC'. Yet, his reputation served as a double-
edged sword. In the words of Myron Meisel,

Once Ulmer was typed as a cheapie director, it became nearly impossible for
him to command any budget whatever, but it was more important to Ulmer
to do his work as he wanted it done than to compromise in the attempt to
mount more expensive productions.[23]

If there is any truth to the old Hollywood adage that you're only as
good as your last movie, then the PRC years did not do much to
boost the status of an offbeat independent director. In fact, Ulmer
appears to have served a rather lengthy sentence in what is sometimes
called 'movie jail', that no-man's land outside the Hollywood
mainstream, where big studios do not deign to look for their
directors. Apart from *Detour*, there are only a handful of films –
foremost among them *Ruthless* (1948), his '*Citizen Kane* in

miniature', featuring the star talent of Zachary Scott and Sidney Greenstreet, and *The Naked Dawn* (1955), his romantic Mexican Western shot in Technicolor, which served as the inspiration for Truffaut's *Jules et Jim* (*Jules and Jim*, 1962) – in which Ulmer was able to realise his full potential as a director, and even then, he never managed to work with a sizeable budget.

Chicken salad out of chicken shit

Detour was budgeted at $87,579.75 – and came in eventually at $117,226.80, a figure that is far higher than the paltry sums often associated with the film ($30,000 in several accounts) – giving it possibly the smallest production budget in the entire canon of classic film noir. To put this into perspective, the shooting of the infamous 'death-house sequence' in Billy Wilder's *Double Indemnity* (1944), bankrolled by Paramount and kept from the final cut of the picture, reportedly cost more than *Detour*'s entire budget.[24] The number of shooting days is often cited as six – most accounts, including those given by people on the set, corroborate this claim – but the final budget lists the total at fourteen in the studio, perhaps merely to allow for any extra days that might have proven necessary, plus four on location. By Ulmer's own account, arguably as unreliable as Al Roberts's voice-over narration, the film was, like most of his others made for PRC, shot in six days, and he was given 15,000 feet of film stock and a shooting ratio of 'two to one, nothing more'. Often cast in heroic terms, Ulmer was sometimes thought to possess, like the Grimm Brothers' 'Rumpelstilzchen', the ability to turn straw into gold, or, as John Landis puts it, in Michael Palm's documentary *Edgar G. Ulmer: Man Off-Screen* (2004), to create 'chicken salad out of chicken shit'.[25] This meant among other things: splicing together short ends; maximising stock footage; borrowing sets from other directors; using his fingers, in lieu of a slate, to count off a scene; and fitting as much as he possibly could into a single take, with very few retakes. Ann Savage insists, for example, 'I don't even recall any retakes except at the very end, when Tom apparently hadn't studied his lines too well and kept blowing it. But with Edgar, we never had retakes.' According to Savage, Ulmer's technique was to 'do a master shot and then come in and take close-ups'.[26] There was not a lot of room for error, or if there were errors, they would have to remain buried in the final cut. As Tim Pulleine has remarked in his re-evaluation of the picture in *Films and Filming*, *Detour* 'could surely be adduced as a prime exhibit in defence of André Gide's dictum that art is born of constraint and dies of freedom'.[27]

Of course, certain aspects of the film's minimalist aesthetic have to do with the way in which Ulmer chose to adapt Goldsmith's story. As Eddie Muller puts it,

Ulmer's vision was to transform the rambling roadside saga into a head-trip: The action is literally confined to what's roiling around in Al Roberts's mind. The bulk of screen time is consumed with tortured close-ups of Tom Neal, pondering his miserable luck in the ultimate 'why me?' voice-over.[28]

Though Muller may overstate the case, Ulmer's heavy use of close-ups and voice-over, not altogether unlike his manipulation of stock footage and rear projection, was without question more than a mere stylistic choice or generic convention. It was what he could do to

The Break O'Dawn Club

give the film a relatively stylish feel – admittedly, with plenty of glimpses of its threadbare or non-existent sets – without breaking the bank.

A telling example of Ulmer's attempt to employ cost-saving measures while still remaining attentive to style and atmosphere is contained in a brief sequence, not long after the film shifts into flashback at the counter of the Reno diner, when Al and Sue leave the Break O'Dawn Club and venture out into the night. Ulmer has Benjamin Kline's camera zero in one last time on the club's neon sign just before it fades to black – an allusion, perhaps, to the murky quality of Al's memory and a faint reminder of the indefinite location, taken in place of a more precise, more expensive shot of an actual locale. Kline then captures Al and Sue, in a fog-filled shot, on the club's steps as they begin their nocturnal stroll. When Al asks Sue if she'd like to grab a bite, she cannot hide her sense of disgust, her loss of appetite the result of working in a 'fleabag' like the Break O'Dawn; at that same moment, filmed against a hazy background, we discern the contours of a man putting out the trash. Al and Sue continue on in what appears to be a blanket of thick fog – 'the B-director's best friend', as Gregory Mank has remarked – masking the exact features of the

Street sign as ersatz film set

Publicity still of Al and Vera posing under a New York City lamppost, far from their actual West Coast destination

neighbourhoods they supposedly traverse and thereby sparing 'an entire costly urban exterior set of New York City'.[29] As they stroll uptown from the club's assumed neighbourhood (in Ulmer's rendition, Greenwich Village – or, as Goldsmith's novel has it, on West 57th Street 'not far from Columbus Circle'), Ulmer maintains the pace by using a series of wipes and by offering several subtle images (a shot of horse-drawn carriages outside Central Park) and a few less-than-subtle ones (close-ups of the street signs along Riverside Drive), combined with the continuation of off-screen dialogue, as a means of hinting at the route they are taking. 'This is how Ulmer spares himself the construction of a set,' asserts Austrian film critic and Ulmer biographer Stefan Grissemann. '*Detour* takes place in a bleak, abstract world.'[30] Curiously, a publicity still from the film has Al and Vera enjoying a smoke under the 81st St/Riverside Dr sign, even though they are never shown together in New York City.

Ulmer had already explored at great length the strategic use of fog, in the absence of sets, in *Strange Illusion* (1945), another PRC cheapie that was released just months before he began work on *Detour*. As Jimmy Lydon, the lead in *Strange Illusion*, has remarked of Ulmer, 'he knew what you could get without exposing a set you didn't have; he knew how to make a two-wall set look like a whole room'.[31] In his short essay, 'Remembering PRC', film historian William K. Everson observes,

My own recollection of the PRCs (confirmed by more recent reviewings) is how dank and dark most of them were. Interior sets were often so threadbare that the lighting was deliberately kept low to hide the fact that there was really nothing to look at. An Edgar Ulmer could answer the challenge and turn darkness into a *film noir* asset, but many directors couldn't.[32]

Or in Bogdanovich's more rhapsodic summation, 'What he could do with nothing . . . remains an object lesson for those directors, myself included, who complain about tight budgets and schedules.'[33] When Sue finally announces, in front of a building we must assume is her apartment, 'Well, here we are,' an echo of the announcement made by the anonymous driver in the film's prologue, it is clear that another journey has been cut short. Only in this case it is a journey to the marriage altar that is rebuffed by Sue, who instead has her own plans ('I want to try my luck in Hollywood'), sans Al, mapped out.

The jackpot

This sequence is immediately succeeded by another scene culminating in a follow-up exchange (more of a monologue, in fact) between Al and Sue – yet another revealing instance of severely limited resources and how these same limitations affect not only the economy of style, and the overall look of the picture, but also its

Stock footage of telephone operators

narrative. As Al stoically, almost defiantly, sits at his piano, banging out a cacophonous medley, from Brahms to boogie-woogie and back to a dissonant waltz (we merely observe a pair of frenetic hands, allegedly belonging to composer Leo Erdody himself,[34] and Al's expressionless face), he is told by a waiter, who brings him an unexpected tip, that he's 'hit the jackpot this time. Ten bucks.' Al's voice-over counters any misplaced glee and betrays his inner scepticism: 'So when this drunk handed me a ten spot after a request, I couldn't get very excited. What was it? I asked myself. A piece of paper crawling with germs. It couldn't buy anything *I* wanted.' But Roberts quickly realises that this might just be his ticket to Sue. He beelines for a phone booth and places a call to Los Angeles, depicted by Ulmer through the canny use of stock footage of telephone operators connecting a maze of phone lines, and then several travelling shots of phone poles against a pastoral backdrop. When Al finally gets Sue on the line, we never hear her speak. Instead, we are left to make out the conversation from Al's comments alone: 'Oh, baby, it's good to hear from you, too!' or 'Me, too, darling' or, still later, 'That's the stuff. That's what I've been wanting to hear you say.' When Al learns that Sue is working as a 'hash-slinger', he retorts with a line that could easily have been spoken by the film's director, 'Those guys out in Hollywood don't know the real thing when it's right in front of them.' We assume that Sue is speaking on the other end of the line, though we never have any definitive proof of that. During one of Al's pauses, we see Sue seated on an upholstered chair, phone receiver against her ear, but she remains silent (a scene that will later be inverted, when Al calls Sue from the squalid room he shares with Vera, and he is unable to utter a word after she answers the phone). Like other instances in the film, this may simply be a case of Al Roberts articulating what's in his head rather than what actually occurred, with the effect of rendering events ever more elliptical.

Even during a relatively cursory first viewing, but especially on closer inspection, the film is rife with basic flaws, breaks in continuity, and blemishes that were never excised or reshot. Take, for example, the scene of Roberts hitchhiking in the desert. We first see him walking along, on the right side of the road, as American traffic conventions would dictate. But then, in a twenty-second sequence, spliced in without any real recourse to continuity, Roberts has moved to the left side, and traffic is visibly driving as if the Mojave Desert suddenly belonged to the British Commonwealth. Ulmer presumably did not detect this until it was

Al thumbing a ride on the right side of the road

An inverted negative, cars driving on the left side of the road

Al hitches lefty

too late to correct, though it might be a sign of a director, so some have claimed, who was willing to allow himself the leeway to sneak in a small prank here and there, especially if it would help increase the chances of keeping his budget in the black.[35] Ironically, during this same brief sequence, when the inverted negative has Roberts sticking out his wrong thumb – both literally and figuratively – the voice-over, in one of its many sympathy-seeking utterances, addresses the viewer directly regarding the tortured predicament of the hitchhiker:

Ever done any hitchhiking? It's not much fun, believe me. Oh yeah, I know all about how it's an education, and how you get to meet a lot of people and all that. But me, from now on, I'll take my education in college or in P.S. 62, or I'll send a dollar ninety-eight in stamps for ten easy lessons.

As if synchronised with the image, the off-screen voice ends its discourse on hitchhiking at the precise moment that Roberts resumes his act of thumbing a ride in the proper direction.

Body for blackmail

A far less detectable imperfection comes later, when Al first encounters Vera hitchhiking in front of a gas station. Al addresses her with a brusque offer to give her a lift ('Hey you! Come on, if you want a ride'), and Vera approaches the car steadily and deliberately, captured in a reverse tracking shot that helps to convey her 'sexual knowingness', as one critic has offered.[36] As she gets into the car through the passenger side, we see, for a fleeting second, that her sweater is noticeably pinned – a means of tightening it and thereby endowing her with more sex appeal – straight up her back. Ulmer allegedly insisted on this wardrobe alteration, so that the curves of Vera's figure could be accentuated, no doubt to heighten the

Vera's sweater pinned up her back

prurient nature of the roadside pick-up. We recall from Al's exchange with Haskell that the kind of girls who hitch rides are not 'Sunday school teachers'. As Ann Savage explains in an interview from 1996,

he [Ulmer] took my sweater and he pulled it real tight and he had the wardrobe woman take this big lap of wool in the back and pin it from the neck down to the bottom of the sweater. And then he said, 'Don't turn around.' And as a matter of fact, when Vera starts to get into that car I caught sight of it [i.e. upon re-watching the film]. You could see a little bit of it and I knew what it was, but I'm sure it wasn't picked up by anybody else.[37]

Indeed, the tawdry, unrefined nature of the film is reflected in the characterisation of its protagonists. Ann Savage's Vera, in particular, is unlike any other femme fatale of the era, far less polished, less beautiful, much more aggressive. As James Naremore remarks of Vera, 'A sullen, dangerous, yet sympathetic figure, she leaves an indelible impression, and it is impossible to imagine any A-budget picture that would have been allowed to depict her.'[38] Savage herself tells how Ulmer insisted, upon viewing the saccharine, dolled-up style that the hair and make-up artists had initially confected for her, that she have dollops of cold cream streaked through her mane to give it a grimy look and, for the same effect, plenty of dirty-brown toner applied to her face. She had to reflect the look of someone who, in Al's words, had 'been thrown off the crummiest freight train in the world'. Coached by Ulmer to spit out her lines with extraordinary velocity as if shot from a 12-gauge rifle – and made hoarse in the process – Vera sounds pretty much like she looks. 'Her voice is shrill, harsh, punishing,' notes one critic, 'a complete explosion of every notion the audience of her day would have had of what a leading lady in a feature film was supposed to sound like.'[39]

Rather defiantly, Ulmer chose to break with industry convention – quite severely, in this case, as Joseph I. Breen's Production Code Administration memo insisted, in no uncertain terms, that in the portrayal of Vera, 'it should be established *affirmatively* that she is a crook and *not* a prostitute'. While Ulmer does not necessarily depict Vera as a prostitute, her putatively lascivious, transgressive behaviour – 'Women *never* hitchhiked rides,' explained Ann Savage in retrospect – exceeds that of her counterparts in the big-studio noirs subjected to greater scrutiny, and the highly sexualised nature of her character leaves the question at the very least ambiguous. Moreover, the publicity materials for the film, in particular the poster art – some of them featuring such racy taglines as 'I used my body for BLACKMAIL' and an 'Adults Only' warning –

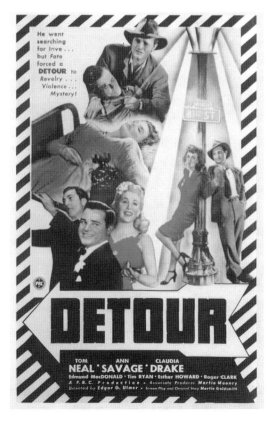

Poster art for the film, with Vera striking the pose of a working girl

A racy publicity still of Vera removing Al's jacket

have Vera leaning against a lamppost smoking and striking a pose, in a 'clingy dress and ankle straps', that, so one critic has argued, replicates the body language of a lady of the night.[40] (Another publicity still has Vera suggestively removing Al's jacket.) The Breen memo goes on to decry any sexual innuendo that might crop up in the film, given the fraught nature of the story: 'It is essential that Alex [Al] and Vera do *not* register as man and wife, and that they be shown living in different apartments. There should be, of course, no suggestion of a sex affair between them.'[41] Of course, they do register as Mr and Mrs Haskell; they do share an apartment; and there are plenty of suggestions of sex – from their fiery exchange about the folding bed to the various bits of chatter laced with erotic overtones – most of them emanating from Vera. As Savage has commented on her uncommonly forward advances as Vera, 'That

Vera's forward pass

A frustrated retreat to the bedroom, sans Al

was an overt motion there, not subtle anymore . . . when she gets up to go to bed, she's quite drunk and she reaches over to touch his shoulder and he really rejects her. It's a real rebuff and this infuriates her.'[42]

While at PRC, Ulmer arguably had more directorial liberty than he would have had at a larger studio, and as a result was in a better position to elude certain restrictions. This does not, however, mean that he was able to sidestep the dictates of the Production Code altogether. To be sure, in his memo of 1 November 1944, Breen stipulates several changes in order to comply with the provisions of the Production Code. The first on his list has to do with the final scene of the film, Al walking alone on the dark highway, and the unwelcome possibility of allowing this scene to intimate, in a considerable violation of Breen's strict moral code, Al's ability to avoid punishment for his sins:

It is absolutely essential that at the end of this story Alex be in the hands of the police, possibly having been picked up by a highway police-car as he was hitchhiking. The concluding narration by Alex's voice should be along the lines that he wonders if all the true facts concerning his troubles will come to light, and what the law will do to him.

What the film delivers in its finished form amounts, for the most part, to a seemingly reluctant acquiescence to Breen's demands.

Seated at the counter of the Reno diner, shrouded once more in darkness except for the partial illumination of his eyes, and still engaged in his lengthy flashback narration, Al tells the final bit of his extended saga:

But my problems weren't solved. I had to stay away from New York – for all time – because Al Roberts was listed as dead and had to stay dead. And I could never go back to Hollywood. Someone might recognise me as Haskell ... Then, too, there was Sue. I could never go to her with a thing like this hanging over my head. All I could do was pray she was happy ...

As Al expresses his wish for Sue's happiness, he gets up and leaves the diner, entering back into the night. Yet, for a brief moment, it appears that Al's shaky confidence is temporarily restored. He strolls a few paces, lights up a cigarette and resumes the voice-over narration – a monologue that was added to the screenplay – giving the fleeting impression that he might just get away with it:

I was in Bakersfield before I read that Vera's body was discovered, and that the police were looking for Haskell in connection with his wife's murder. Isn't that a laugh? Haskell got me into this mess, and Haskell was getting me out of it. The police were searching for a dead man.

The film, however, does not end here. Instead, Al continues to walk along the highway, his thoughts shifting in tenor toward the more righteous. The shift begins with his return to the same impulse to forget, to 'cut away a piece of your memory or blot it out', as he describes it at the start of his protracted flashback. He can't help but wonder how his life might have turned out had he never stepped into Haskell's car. However, Al's predominant sense of uncertainty, running throughout much of the film and informing his many rationalisations, is countered by a sudden torrent of unequivocality: 'But one thing I don't have to wonder about ... I *know*. ...' The final segment of the epilogue, triggered

by Al's realisation that there is no way to get off scott-free, is a
startling, rather inconsonant moment of clarity that clashes with
the overriding moral ambiguity of the film. His oft-quoted final
line of voice-over narration ('Some day a car will stop to pick me
up that I never thumbed . . . Yes, fate or some mysterious force can
put the finger on you or me for no good reason at all') is, in the
end, a more artful way of saying that Al Roberts cannot escape the
law, and Joseph I. Breen says so.

I can't believe that you're in love with me
Among the many choices that Ulmer and his film crew would have to
make in order to mitigate any financial excesses was the decision to
replace the original theme song, Duke Ellington's 'Sophisticated
Lady', with 'I Can't Believe that You're in Love with Me', a Tin Pan
Alley number written by Clarence Gaskill and Jimmy McHugh.
This move took the narrative in a different direction and, according
to the official production budget, also cut $2,000 off the bottom line.
The removal of 'Sophisticated Lady', which remained ensconced in
Goldsmith's screenplay – and was allegedly kept in the works all the
way into the final shooting script[43] – meant replacing a classic jazz
standard with a song that had in the 30s been quite popular, but by
the release of the film was very much a thing of the past. As Caryl
Flynn has argued in her critical study of film music, the inclusion of
such a song helps to call attention to the regressive nature of Al's
fantasy and his obsessive focus on the past.[44] Whereas 'Sophisticated
Lady' might be read as a song that would shed light onto Sue's
perspective ('They say into your early life romance came/And this
heart of yours burned a flame/A flame that flickered one day and died
away,/Then, with disillusion deep in your eyes,/you learned that fools
in love grow wise'), the lyrics of 'I Can't Believe that You're in Love
with Me' are much more an extension of Al's self-pitying
predicament. Alone, the refrain ('Your eyes of blue/Your kisses too,/I
never knew what they could do,/I can't believe that you're in love
with me') evokes Al's helplessness, whereas the final lines of the song

Al and Sue playing their song at the Break O'Dawn Club

serve to heighten that sense and, visually, are reflected in the film, as Sue stands over Al while playing *their* song ('I have always placed you far above me,/I just can't imagine that you love me;/And after all is said and done,/To think that I'm the lucky one,/I can't believe that you're in love with me').

Lest we forget, it is precisely that tune ('Why was there always that rotten tune!') that, to paraphrase one of Al's earliest voice-overs, follows him around, beats in his head and never lets up – to be sure, 'that rotten tune' is what causes Al's initial outburst and sends the story into flashback. Thus, 'I Can't Believe . . .' becomes his own mantra, haunting him and reminding him of the paradise that he once ostensibly had and that is now irretrievably lost. Al may well try to forget, to repress his dark past along with his tormented memories, but they inevitably surge to the surface with relentless force, transmitted as it were by the strains of an otherwise pleasant, easy-listening song ('The first good piece played tonight,' as the man behind the counter at the Nevada diner protests. 'Some people just ain't got any good taste'). Ironically, by cutting the cost of using the Duke Ellington number, Ulmer ends up with a song that better encapsulates the agony of Al Roberts, the single story he opts to tell, and the bleakness of the film as a whole.

Too little of it

Finally, the low-budget nature of *Detour* – the acute self-consciousness vis-à-vis money – is something that, rather essentially if also belatedly, gets worked in to the script. For example, the pointed commentary on money that comes soon after Al heads out west is a complete add-on to the screenplay, perhaps by Ulmer, perhaps by Mooney, perhaps a variation on Goldsmith's original. It is, in any case, a notable moment in a film by a director who once famously claimed, 'I really am looking for absolution for all the things I had to do for money', and who was especially fearful of being 'ground up in the Hollywood hash machine'.

Money. You know what that is. It's the stuff you never have enough of. Little green things with George Washington's picture that men slave for, commit crimes for, die for. It's the stuff that has caused more trouble in the world than anything else we ever invented, simply because there's too little of it. At least I had too little of it. So it was me for the thumb.

As the director, by then only on a one-year contract at PRC, Ulmer needed no reminding of the studio's lack of money. Throughout his career, he hustled to make ends meet, eking out a living by showing unremitting resourcefulness and little sense of financial entitlement (Ulmer's director fee for *Detour*, as listed on the official PRC budget, was a mere $750 – the equivalent of less than $9,000 today). In a sense, then, like Al Roberts, he had to thumb his way through the production, taking lifts here and there, cheating his way with an occasional short cut when the straight and narrow just wouldn't do.

In addition to the commentary in Ulmer's *Detour*, we have in Goldsmith's novel a similar discourse on money that, despite a shared turn of phrase uttered moments earlier in the film, gives things a slightly different spin. In the words of Alexander Roth:

They say that money is nothing, that a buck is only a piece of paper crawling with germs, and that you can't buy happiness with cash. I say sour grapes.

Name one thing money can't buy. Respect? That's usually the first item people mention. Well, will you tell me who respects a guy *without* money? A guy that's starving, say, or on the bum? Go on the bum sometime and find out how much respect you get. I know. Love? That's usually the next come-back. Brother, don't ever let anyone pull that on you. You can win a woman a lot easier with a mink coat than with poetry and walks in the park.

Taken together, these two commentaries call attention to the overwrought value of money in American culture of the late 30s and 40s, in the wake of the Great Depression and the Second World War. They also both self-consciously play off of the pitched battle between art and commerce, of having too little or even too much (as Roberts puts it, after he gains possession of the $768 in Haskell's wallet: 'This was a lot of jack – but believe me, it was the kind of money I'd rather not have'). As German director Wim Wenders remarks in Michael Palm's 2004 documentary, commenting on the severe lack of resources Ulmer often faced: 'You always think that one needs a lot of money to make films. But in the end, the more money you have, the less you can do with it.' Without the cushion of a generous budget, so Wenders claims, one is forced to compensate with 'camerawork, ideas, abstraction', and 'to invent the picture when you cannot afford it'.

4 In Search of Meaning

In spite of its inherently suspicious take on American capitalism and on Hollywood of the 40s – with its doom-and-gloom storyline and bold array of brutal imagery – *Detour* received favourable reviews in the local trade papers when it was first released. The *Hollywood Reporter* pronounced it 'an excellent picture' and 'the best film PRC has ever produced', asserting further that the overall 'achievement is unmistakably attributable to Ulmer'.[45] Although less effusive in its praise (calling the film 'adequate as second half of a double bill'), *Variety* was quick to point out that 'Director Edgar Ulmer manages to keep the show smartly paced', while a review in *Film Daily* highlighted the 'suspense and vividness' that Ulmer was able to achieve with the picture and gave the direction and photography a rating of 'good'.[46] Finally, in one of the few notices in the popular press, a critic for the *Los Angeles Times* called *Detour*,

One of the most poignant and disturbing stories to reach the screen in any year is this one. You're not just looking at a picture; you're right in it and suffering along with the man whose troubles are being told . . . no mere recital of the tale can convey its painful verisimilitude. Direction is tops, with no opportunity overlooked.[47]

Given Ulmer's marginal status in the world of Hollywood, and given the second-class standing of a Poverty Row studio like PRC, who could have expected more attention?

In the many years since, what may have once been missing in the way of critical attention has been lavished upon the film, which is to say that *Detour* has been reinterpreted and reappraised from innumerable angles, with the added benefit of new scholarship, new sources and new methods. Rather than rehearsing each and every interpretation of the film that has appeared since 1945, let me instead highlight a few cornerstones, fleshing things out where necessary and pointing to several of the more incisive readings by contemporary scholars and critics. My focus will be centred primarily on those interpretations that emerged after the first wave of auteurism was on the wane, when the emphasis on formal style and the signature stamp of a director shifted to include narrative, genre and historical context. This should provide the chance to address some of the chief analytic quandaries, enigmas and assorted tales from the trenches of production that have occasionally left viewers flummoxed and sent scholars on the hunt for plausible answers.

Male fantasies

Much of *Detour* is about seeing, and seeing from the vantage point of Al Roberts, in particular, starting from that artfully illuminated gaze rendered in close-up as Ulmer has us track in on – or, really, tunnel into – his subjective state of torment. All we see during the series of extended flashbacks are Al's projections. At least that's what several critics have argued, none perhaps more forcefully than Tania Modleski in her essay 'Film Theory's Detour'. Cast in a feminist psychoanalytic framework, Modleski's approach examines Ulmer's

The artfully illuminated gaze, signalling the shift into flashback

film in terms of male anxiety and hostility. For her, the early scene of Sue announcing her plans to leave for Hollywood conjures up the image of 'a child being abandoned by its mother'. (The only overt reference in the film we have to Al's mother – more of an idiomatic expression than a symbolic reference – is when Al, warding off the unsolicited small talk of an over-garrulous trucker at the Reno diner, snaps, 'My mother taught me never to talk to strangers.')

What follows, then, in Modleski's reading of Al's cross-country journey is a re-enactment of a profound yearning to be reunited with the 'mother'. Sue serves as an untenable fantasy of 'good mother', while Vera in her role of 'bad mother' is, so the argument goes, 'a projection of the male's own bad impulses'.[48] These countervailing images are most poignantly depicted in scenes built around mirror reflections, thus underscoring the subjective nature of Al's projections.

The first case in point is when Al takes to the wheel while driving with Haskell, and he looks into his rear-view mirror, a stylishly framed image that quickly dissolves to Sue singing in front of three shadow musicians – an embellishment that Ulmer seems to have borrowed from Arthur Robison's foray into expressionist lighting in *Schatten: Eine nächtliche Halluzination* (*Warning Shadows: A Nocturnal Hallucination*, 1923). Driving through the night and becoming increasingly groggy, thus more susceptible to dreaming, Al suddenly feels uncharacteristically upbeat, imagining that he will soon join Sue in California. He begins to think of the future, which, in his words, 'couldn't have been brighter if I'd embroidered it with neon lights'. He then announces, in a statement that will prove to be little more than a flight of fancy, 'it was nice to think of Sue shooting to the top'. When the mirror frame finally dilates and opens up on Sue, she is once more singing their song, this time in a shimmering sequin gown – distinct from the comparatively unremarkable black ball-gown she wears in Al's first memory of her – and is very much the star of the show. Ironically, Al's last off-screen line leading into the sequence suggests his tacit awareness of the fantasy ('It's amazing what a full belly can do to your imagination'),

Al peers into the rear-view mirror

The shadow fantasy of Sue's glamorous success

when of course the act of looking into the rear-view mirror is an unambiguous backward glance and, in the words of Modleski, 'points up the regressive nature of his journey'. This sequence is essentially self-contained in the rear-view mirror, returning as it does to that same tight frame before finally cutting to Al's more immediate, less rosy reality as the rain begins to intrude and Haskell's impending death is at arm's length.

The second critical scene in Modleski's analysis takes place near the very end of the film, when Al unwittingly strangles Vera, pulling the telephone cord from underneath the door as she threatens to rat him out to the Hollywood police. Our initial exposure to her death is, significantly, given in mirror reflection. Al breaks down the door and

The mirror reflection of Vera's death

finds her lying lifeless on the bed, the phone cord still wrapped around her neck. For Modleski, Vera slamming the door on Al 'parallels the earlier rejection by Sue', but in this case elicits a rage-filled response from Al that is 'a fitting end to a violently played out *fort/da* game initiated by the "mother's" desertion'. (Freud speaks of the 'fort/da game' as a game of disappearance and return – 'fort' in German meaning gone and 'da' meaning here – played by a child who seeks to control his or her anxiety associated with a mother's absence.) In her final analysis, Modleski uses Ulmer's film as a test case, as fallible as it may be, for Hollywood cinema: '*Detour* is remarkable for the clarity with which it demonstrates the truth that in Hollywood cinema women are often nothing but mirror-projections of male fears and male fantasies.'[49] The representation of Vera is indeed far from flattering (Modleski herself calls Vera 'one of the most ferocious persecutory *femme fatales* in the history of cinema'), and is no doubt coloured by Al's skewed perception, but the film's depictions of both her and Sue have less to do with 'Hollywood cinema' than with the fact that they inhabit a turn-and-burn, grimy Poverty Row production. Vera's roughness stems, at least in part, from the material conditions of the film, as does the lack of a more fully developed, independent role for Sue, whose story is severely cut due to the exigencies of a sixty-eight-minute picture.[50] But the fundamental point of Modleski's analysis remains true. Ulmer's film, told from Al's perspective and literally through his own eyes, is saturated with male fantasies and anxieties: from the thrill-laden pick-up of a female hitchhiker to the horror of being held captive; from the precious vision of Al's true love in a glowing spotlight to the nightmare of never reuniting with her after expending all that's left in his soul to reach that untenable destination.

Unreliability

With a sustained concentration on the film's storyline, something auteurist critics had formerly been loath to address ('beneath trash', as one memorably wrote), Andrew Britton's trenchant reading of *Detour* in Ian Cameron's *Book of Film Noir* applies great pressure to the film's narrative cul-de-sacs, its twists and turns, and its sudden digressions. For Britton, beyond the generic significance of the film as a low-budget noir, it is 'one of the most demanding and audacious narratives ever produced in Hollywood'.[51] The periodically misleading, disorienting quality of the story can be traced back to Al's cagey, elliptical and stridently defensive voice-over commentary, which includes several fleeting insights that reveal that even he is aware of his own unreliability – aware that those watching and listening to him will inevitably disbelieve his story; aware that they will bear 'that "Don't-make-me-laugh!" expression' on their 'smug faces'; and aware that they will pin him to a pattern of mendacity of the most incriminating sort. Like the other principal characters in the

The shadowy itinerary of Al's westward trek

film, Al loses control over his itinerary and thus over his fate. When he first witnesses, and possibly contributes to Haskell's death, Al insists, 'From then on, something else stepped in and shunted me off to a different destination than the one I'd picked for myself.' But even well before then, when he first makes his way west, a few quick glimpses of a map on the screen provide us with only the haziest idea of any specific, preconceived route that Al will take. Ulmer presents this by way of montage, an amalgamation of incongruous images, which bestows upon Al's journey a vertiginous quality. First, Ulmer superimposes over the map – the points of which are only vaguely discernible – the shadow of Al's feet marching west; he then intercuts shots of him hitchhiking, with Al's voice-over delivering his impassioned discourse on money, thus highlighting his impoverished state. As John Belton has argued, 'These montages fragment and abstract his linear progress through space. The film provides no arrows or dotted lines, just the unreadable and unread image of the map.'[52]

In *Detour*, there is no 'linear progress' and, in fact, Al's highly fatalistic, not to say defeatist, attitude denies the very notion of progress, of controlling his own destiny or possessing his own free will. 'As far as Al is concerned,' writes Britton,

everything that happens to him is completely arbitrary. He has come to a bad
end because providence assigned him one, and, as he surrenders to the
inevitable, he has at least the comfort of knowing that things would have
turned out much better if he had been left to his own devices.[53]

We recognise this from our very first exposure to Al in the prologue,
when he stumbles in and out of the frame as if being propelled by the
wind, and when he is banging away at the keys after hours at the
Break O'Dawn club while he and Sue have one of their revealing
chats: she compliments Al on his skills as a pianist, likening him to
Polish composer Ignacy Jan Paderewski and suggesting he might
make Carnegie Hall someday, but the spirit of his response is all too
clear, 'Yeah, as the janitor.' For Al, fate will always trip him up,
keeping him from getting what he wants, what he rightfully deserves,
and in his jaded view, there's nothing he can do about it. He is neither
willing to admit his culpability in what transpires over the course of
his story, nor is he able to acknowledge the possible distortions and
elisions of his recollections. Britton compares the unreliable narration
of Al Roberts to the modernist fiction of Henry James (*The Turn of
the Screw et al.*), which leaves behind subtle clues as to the narrator's
tendentious point of view, and to Freud's notion of 'secondary
revision', a potent 'mechanism of unconscious censorship' that invites
repression or other forms of reworking the past as a means of
preventing an honest reckoning with traumatic events.

While Al doggedly attempts to convince himself and the
audience of his story, offering up prevarication after prevarication,
the single figure who will have none of it, and as a result stands in as
the consummate spoiler, is Vera. Rather omnisciently, she sees right
through Al from the very first moment they meet – when she wakes
up from her deceptively short nap and demands, 'Where did you
leave his body?' Vera recognises Al for the schlemiel that he is, the
architect, in no small measure, of his own misfortune. From the
outset, she pelts him with a steady stream of scurrilous banter that
aims to unmask his duplicitous ways and to take the burden off the

'Where did you leave his body?'

shoulders of fate: 'That's the greatest cock-and-bull story I ever heard!' she tells him after he first describes what happened to Haskell. Vera follows this with a litany of insults she tosses like Molotov cocktails: 'Not only don't you have any scruples, you don't have any brains!' and 'Your philosophy stinks!' and 'That's the trouble with you, Roberts! All you do is bellyache.' In the presence of Vera, Al has no choice but to admit his complicity: 'My goose was cooked, she had me,' he laments when Vera first blows his cover; and he echoes this same portentous remark ('I was cooked') when he finally kills her and there's no longer any point trying to wriggle out.

Naturally, Vera is no paragon of reliability. We are never even certain that's her real name ('You can call me Vera, if you like'), and she seems perfectly happy to do whatever it takes – lie, cheat, scratch her way out – to get what she wants. (In Goldsmith's novel, Roth's commentary makes a point, before describing her tragic background, of using the conditional, 'If a person could believe her . . .'.) The key difference between the two is their contrasting level of self-recognition. As Britton notes of Vera, 'Her values may be despicable, but she never pretends, to herself or anyone else, that they are anything but what they are.'[54] At the same time, however, Vera insists to Al that they're both 'born in the same gutter'. Her presence, then, like the presence of Haskell (in a tangible sense, she represents

Haskell's demonic spirit), serves as a foil against which Al's passivity, his lack of a stiff backbone and his propensity to surrender his destiny to external forces are all amplified. Already in their initial dialogue this is made clear, Vera turning Al's question 'How far are you going?' right back on him. When he offers 'Los Angeles' in return, she replies 'LA is good enough for me, mister.' They are locked in from that moment on.

Another feature highlighting Al's unreliability is the way his voice-over narration distinguishes itself from its noir counterparts. Unlike, say, Walter Neff (Fred MacMurray) in Billy Wilder's *Double Indemnity* or Frank Chambers (John Garfield) in Tay Garnett's *The Postman Always Rings Twice*, Al never reveals that he is offering a confession to a specific audience – a superior at work, a priest, some other authority – or even with a specific purpose in mind. Nonetheless, he seems to recognise and anticipate the response of those who may be listening to him and who, inevitably, will doubt what he has to say. This adds to the paranoia and to the hyper-awareness of the narrator, calling attention to the story as such – and to the film as a whole – giving it the self-reflexive quality of metafiction or metacinema. Al is so hell-bent on fashioning his story as the truth that he tries to pit it against a counter example, a sanitised version, or a Hollywood ending in the mould of the forced epilogue to F. W. Murnau's *Der letzte Mann* (*The Last Laugh*, 1924). For example, after the first night that Al and Vera hole up together in Los Angeles, he remarks in his voice-over:

If this were fiction, I would fall in love with Vera, marry her and make a respectable woman of her. Or else she'd make some supreme Class-A sacrifice for me and die. Sue and I would bawl a little over her grave, make some crack about there is good in all of us. But Vera, unfortunately, was just as rotten in the morning as she'd been before.

This artificial contrast serves Al as a means of trumping up his claims to the truth, of presenting his story as a vérité rendering of the brutality of life stripped of its candy coating. (In Goldsmith's novel, the same passage begins 'If this were a movie', and Vera's imagined sacrifice is followed by a more demonstrative critique of the movie industry, noting how such a whitewashing of the story would be tantamount to throwing a bone to 'the Hays office and the morons in the mezzanine'.) Yet Al realises, in the end, that even this may not offset the powerful current of social disbelief. 'The world is full of sceptics,' he utters once he's finally at rock bottom, having just strangled Vera to death. 'I know, I'm one myself.'

Finally, the acute unreliability of the narrator, for whom the truth is merely something the police will laugh at, may have a personal connection with a director who was known off screen for telling many a tall tale. Indeed, like others in his extended cohort of European-born directors in Hollywood (von Stroheim, Preminger, Wilder), Ulmer played an active role in the creation of a fanciful new identity for his transplanted existence. Sometimes called the 'aesthete from the Alps', he liked to fashion himself as a Viennese *Wunderkind* weaned on the classics of music, art, literature and philosophy – and forever unwilling to compromise. Perhaps for him, as for Brecht, mendacity was merely the modus operandi of the business, the peddling of lies a means to an end. Over the years, though, Ulmer's reputation for stretching the truth has not always been granted such understanding; film historian Lotte Eisner once purportedly dismissed him as 'the greatest liar in the history of cinema'.[55]

Allegories of exile

In a 1990 article in *Cahiers du cinéma*, French critic Charles Tesson speculates that the journey of Al Roberts reflects a journey Ulmer himself made from New York to Hollywood a few years earlier. Near the beginning of the film, observes Tesson, at the Break O'Dawn, soon after Sue leaves for Hollywood:

The pianist plays something classical, which after a while turns into a jazz medley and thus brings something to expression that has to do with Ulmer, something that led him on his path from Europe to Hollywood. Al, the pianist at a low-level establishment, may wish to dream of Carnegie Hall just as a PRC director might dream of MGM.[56]

Al's frenzied improvisation of a Brahms waltz, bringing to bear the tension between a high European classical tradition and a popular American blues-based vernacular style, serves as a quintessential moment for Tesson, who hones in on Ulmer's passion for music – indeed his first passion, even above cinema, and a passion that was never entirely fulfilled – and notes the extraordinary role that it plays in the film. In Al's journey back in time, the abrupt shift into flashback comes to him, significantly, via music. The memories that he so ardently tries to repress escape to the surface when he hears the tunes of his past. More broadly speaking, as Austrian film scholar Alexander Horwath has maintained, music figures for Ulmer as a means of highlighting the 'allegories of a typical emigrant situation'.[57] That is to say, it amplifies the tension between the old world and the new, between Brahms and boogie-woogie.[58]

As Edward Said has remarked, 'For an exile, habits of life, expression or activity in the new environment inevitably occur against the memory of these things in another environment. Thus the new and the old environments are vivid, actual, occurring together contrapuntally.'[59] With the help of Erdody, Ulmer handles the film music 'contrapuntally' as a medium for expressing at once Al's tormented state of mind and a virtual exilic state that he may be thought to represent. In certain moments, as in the case Tesson describes, there is an ironic conflation of incongruous European and American styles. Or, in another such instance, the inclusion of the widely played 40s song 'I'm Always Chasing Rainbows', in tandem with the classical composition that serves as its basis, Chopin's *Fantasie Impromptu* in C Sharp Minor, works to underscore the messy distinction and attendant friction between high culture and pop. Just as we can discern a few bars of the song at key junctures in the film (e.g. when Al is in transit), so too can we imagine Al humming the lyrics ('Some fellows look and find the sunshine,/I always look and find the rain').[60] In still other cases, the irony of Ulmer and Erdody's choice of music is more singularly bitter, even mocking. The most obvious example here are the strains of 'Home, Sweet Home', played when Al and Vera take possession of the pair of dingy rooms in Los Angeles that convey anything but home, when the homelessness of the two inhabitants is all too apparent (in fact, each of them utters an ironic repetition of the song's title).

The perceived conflict between classical music and jazz is something that was shared by numerous German-speaking émigrés, perhaps the most vociferous among them Theodor W. Adorno, who saw jazz as a major component in the odious machinery of the culture industry. 'For Adorno, jazz summed up everything that is vulgar and debased in American culture,' remarks Paul Cantor, who goes on to draw the link between the scene that Tesson describes and Adorno's critique of jazz: 'Roberts earns a ten-dollar tip from a nightclub patron for prostituting his art and Brahms's. It almost seems as if Ulmer has been reading Adorno.'[61] Al's performance of a 'sarcastic disfiguration' of Brahms, earning him an instant financial bonus, would seem to confirm this claim, as would his noticeable enmity for the off-screen jazz musician playing his saxophone outside the room he and Vera occupy in Los Angeles; when he first hears the sax, he wishes the saxophonist would just 'give up', while later, after Vera lies dead on her bed, Al senses that he is no longer playing a jazzy 'love song', which was disturbing enough, but a 'dirge'.[62] Cast as the supreme outsider, Al's initial rejection of the once-beloved Tin Pan Alley number 'I Can't Believe that You're in Love with Me' at the Nevada diner elicits not only the dismissive remarks about his lack of taste, but also a wartime defence of American culture and values: 'It's a free country,' the trucker retorts, 'and I can play whatever I want to.' Jazz may have more affirmative attributes attached to it in other Ulmer films (e.g. in *Jive Junction* or even *Carnegie Hall*, his 1947 tribute to musical virtuosity), but in *Detour* it is a harsh reminder of Al's dejected and cheapened condition.

At the California state border inspection

Examining the film in the context in which it appeared in 1945, and also in the context of an émigré director's life, there are other aspects that might further lend themselves to an allegorical reading, to interpreting the film as an oblique commentary on the experience of exile. First and foremost, there is the issue of constant displacement and a severe lack of any kind of permanence. Al Roberts is 'condemned to wander like the Flying Dutchman along the back roads of America', as Bill Krohn emphatically remarks.[63] Like most characters in the film, Al is constantly on the run, crossing state lines, searching for refuge in 'some city', where he will be safe and anonymous. His behaviour mirrors in certain respects the behavioural patterns of exiles, especially as Anthony Heilbut describes them in his magisterial study *Exiled in Paradise*:

Scurrying from place to place, 'changing one's nationality almost as often as one changed one's shoes,' they became adept at subterfuge and chicanery. Law-abiding citizens, now no longer citizens, became cunning outlaws, smuggling currency, property, and people across the borders.[64]

Unlike Goldsmith's Alexander Roth, Al Roberts is not marked as specifically Jewish, and yet he nonetheless bears subtle traits of a *luftmensch* or Wandering Jew. By the end of the film, when Al is stripped of everything, including his own name, he has become 'a veritable exile'.[65]

There is, moreover, a pervasive sense of homelessness in all characters in the film.[66] We see no families, no children, no links to a larger, more stable community. In Grissemann's apt summation:

Ulmer hands over his characters to a labyrinth of bars, motel rooms and highway rest stops – to anonymous spaces that could be anywhere – or to a nowhere, a world for nothing and nobody. The locales of *Detour* are way stations, places of passage. Everything else Ulmer boldly eliminates. In contrast to Goldsmith's novel, his *film noir* gets by without any proper home, without living or private quarters.[67]

The 'contrapuntal' dimension of the exile experience, as Said describes it, may be traced back to the homeless condition and what this lack of home means in the new world. As Thomas Elsaesser puts it,

The story of the German film émigrés . . . presupposes a twofold estrangement: from their own home, and from the view that their American hosts had of this homeland. The consequence of this was a kind of schizophrenia, which, in turn also gave a double perspective on American society – one of admiration and the other a hyper-critical view, both perspectives vying with one another.[68]

Like the two competing kinds of music, these two perspectives come into a productive conflict in *Detour*, where the sum effect is not so much to evoke the 'loneliness of man without God', as Luc Moullet once suggested as the overarching theme in Ulmer, but rather the loneliness of the individual – émigré, exile and native-born alike. It is, indeed, a loneliness that is historically conditioned by the war, migration, the Great Depression and the profound loss of hope felt by many wanderers, drifters and refugees during the specific moment chronicled in the film.

The man who wasn't there

One of the lingering interpretive quandaries concerning *Detour* has
nothing at all to do with its formal composition. Nor does it concern
the basis of the film's story and its various influences or its possible
bearing on the life and career of its director. Rather, this particular
enigma has to do with bookkeeping, or, more specifically, with a name
that appears on the PRC budget under director – *not* Ulmer's name.
Just above the notation of E. Ulmer, which is also relegated to the space
allotted for the director and is assigned a $750 fee, is a certain
L. Landers carrying a director fee of $3,000. Lew Landers (né Louis
Friedlander) was a well-known figure around PRC, having directed
two other films for the company in the same year as *Detour*: first,
Crime, Inc., based on a novel by *Detour*'s associate producer Martin
Mooney (who also served as associate producer for Landers) and co-
starring Tom Neal; and second, *Shadow of Terror*, a film whose release
date preceded the release of *Detour* by a mere few weeks. Like Ulmer,
Landers began his career at Universal, directing such films as the
Lugosi–Karloff vehicle *The Raven* (1935), shortly after Ulmer himself
had made his debut at the studio with the Lugosi–Karloff vehicle *The
Black Cat*. And also like Ulmer, Landers gained a reputation in the 40s
as someone who could turn out decent second-billers on the cheap,
directing in some years, such as 1945, upwards of eight feature films.

How Landers's name wound up on the PRC production budget
– and allegedly is the sole name listed on the original shooting script
for the film – is really anyone's guess. The fact that it appears there at
all has prompted some critics, such as Pierre Rissient, to seize the
opportunity to play devil's advocate and to deny Ulmer's involvement
altogether. As Rissient has provocatively remarked, 'You know, of
course, Ulmer didn't direct *Detour*.'[69] This kind of flippant assertion,
taken as somehow self-evident by its source, may come off as a
wicked joke to Rissient's former associates at *Cahiers du cinéma*,
who were indeed among the first to view the film as Ulmer's *chef
d'oeuvre*, but it doesn't do much in the way of explaining the odd
presence of Lew Landers's name on the budget.

The lack of a proper explanation has, however, been treated more seriously by other scholars and critics of late. Stefan Grissemann probes the question of Landers's presence in his biography of Ulmer: 'Does he serve as a straw man in order to legitimize granting a PRC film of this size such an unusually high director fee? Is it a simple transcription error about which nobody seemed to care whether or not it be deleted?'[70] Bookkeeping at Poverty Row studios was notoriously shady, and if having Landers's name on the budget allowed Fromkess and his money men to move around funds in a form of creative accounting, or if the transcription of Landers's name is merely one of possibly many such errors, so be it. In his more recent analysis, Robert Polito enquires as to whether Landers's fee for *Shadow of a Doubt* 'was absorbed into the *Detour* budget'.[71] The exact details will likely never be known. Yet the temptation to speculate, to imagine, for instance, that Ulmer never had a hand in what has come to be identified as his signature production can only go so far. 'The one thing that is certain', asserts Grissemann, 'is that Lew Landers had nothing to do with the shooting of *Detour*. Nobody who experienced the shoot ever spoke of a second director.'[72] Of the surviving members of the cast, the only one who has had the chance to weigh in on this question is Ann Savage, who knew Landers from his *Two-Man Submarine*, 'a waterlogged wartime adventure' he made for Columbia in 1944, in which she and Neal had played opposite each other. In her words: 'Lew was an old friend, and I liked him a lot. But I never saw him anywhere near *Detour*. It was always Edgar.'[73]

5 And the Sky was Grey

Perhaps the most common interpretive lens through which to
examine *Detour* is film noir, that elusive term – a style, a mood, an
epoch or, for some, a bona fide film genre – that the French began to
apply to American film in the mid-40s, very soon after the release of
Ulmer's film. There is good reason for this, given that *Detour* bears
undeniable affinities with many of the stock attributes (cynicism,
pessimism and darkness) and generic conventions (flashback
narration, low-key lighting, the pairing of a femme fatale with a
down-trodden male anti-hero) frequently associated with film noir.[74]
Yet, there are also notable differences in *Detour*'s adherence to any
sort of standard template, and depending on which definition of this
notoriously ill-defined term one chooses to employ, *Detour* may
prove to be *sui generis*. The one approach that seems especially
germane, and not overly restrictive, is Raymond Borde and Etienne
Chaumeton's discussion in *Panorama du film noir Americain* (1955),
which sees film noir, in John Belton's rendering, as 'a purely affective
phenomenon – that is, it disturbs viewers; it disorients them; it
produces a profound uneasiness in audiences'.[75] True enough.
Yet, even so, the limitations of the term film noir are revealed in the
broad-ranging critical reception of *Detour*, in which there is little
general agreement.

As screenwriter Hossein Amini has said of the film, 'the label
film noir doesn't do justice to the sheer blackness that pervades its
story'. For Amini, what is noir about *Detour* comes across much
more in the human vulnerability of its characters than the style in
which the film is presented.

It's not the lighting or the framing, or the fog that make *Detour* a true *film noir*,
it's the bleak romantic sensibility running through it. . . . The *noir* was in the

characters' hearts and in their relationships, not just in the shadows on the streets.[76]

To be sure, unlike many – though certainly not all – classic noirs, *Detour* has very few scenes that take place in the city streets, and those that do are either shrouded in fog or merely shot against a projected backdrop. The spaces so typical of film noir are largely absent. This may have to do with the poverty of the production, making *Detour* distinct from A-class vehicles. Goldsmith is said to have remarked in an interview, long after *Detour*'s release, '*Film noir*, film schnor. The whole idea was film cheap.'[77] The cheapness, then, gives the film a different feel – possibly a different *Weltanschauung* – that resists standard interpretations of noir. As Richard Combs has put it, 'the mood of *Detour*, in the end, is more *noir et bleu*, its grainy little puzzles of identity swamped, again, by dialogue which asserts a considerably more beaten-up view of the world'.[78] Rather than belabour the precise classification of something as imprecise as film noir, let us instead turn to a few different ways of reading *Detour* against the grain, not disputing entirely that it is indeed a noir, but recognising the true malleability of such generic tags.

Film gris

The term film gris was first introduced in 1985 by Thom Andersen as a means of describing the 'often drab and depressing' films made by leftist directors (Abraham Polonsky, Joseph Losey, Jules Dassin, Nicholas Ray, among others) in the late 40s and 50s. According to Andersen, these directors tried to achieve 'greater psychological and social realism' than their counterparts in film noir; they also displayed greater awareness of class conflict and of 'the unreality of the American dream'.[79] While Ulmer would not immediately fit into the taxonomy that Andersen develops – though he did go on, in 1948, to work on *Ruthless* with blacklisted writer Alvah Bessie – *Detour* can be seen to reflect many of the attributes of film gris.

As Dana Polan has persuasively argued in a 2002 reconsideration of
Detour in *Senses of Cinema*:

The *films gris* reject *noir* glamour and wallow instead in an unremitting
bleakness. Where romantic *film noir* pictures a world of larger-than-life
figures, the *films gris* deal with all-too-average losers, everyday American
citizens who are caught in the rat race of dead-end career options and
desperately try to beat the system by means that are as meagre as their
dreams. In *Detour*, it is important that Al Roberts's journey propels him
westward toward Los Angeles and the radiant blondeness of his girlfriend
Sue. In a parody of the foundational American myth of the pioneer quest, Al's
'Mecca' turns out to be a hopeless site of broken dreams, lost illusions.[80]

In *Detour*, Al's journey may begin as a subtle variation on a classical
American myth, the Horace Greeley story of westward migration, but
it almost instantaneously undoes that same myth. As Andersen puts it,
in reference to another film (Losey's *The Prowler* of 1951), we observe
a 'vision of upward mobility . . . gone sour'.[81] In basic agreement with
the general attitude of film gris, Ulmer's film does not depict wealthy,
romantic heroes, but rather working-class stiffs and other run-of-the-
mill hacks. When Al begins his trek, before he lands a ride with
Haskell, he is seen seated next to an American farmer, almost a spin-
off of Grant Wood's 'American Gothic', and then next to another,
more anonymous man of the West in a woody station wagon.
These fleeting profiles are presented as prototypical American folkloric
figures extracted from the 40s landscape, figures who, like the lonely
trucker at the Nevada diner near the start of the picture, have a deep
Depression-era glaze in their eyes.[82] In this respect, 'Ulmer identified an
emptiness in the heart of America', as George Lipsitz has argued, and
he did so without any studio gloss, merely with a couple of shots
interspersed into one of the most incongruous segments of the film.[83]

Quite different from the more sumptuously designed film noirs,
Detour does not take place in 'swanky nightclubs' or in 'overblown
apartments or mansions'. Instead, the audience is introduced to a

Ulmer's riff on 'American Gothic'

Al with a man of the West in a woody station wagon

string of low-level establishments, starting with the Nevada diner in which Al begins and ends his elaborate saga, and continuing on through the Break O'Dawn Club, the truck stop where Al and Haskell stop for a bite, the highway motel, the LA flophouse, the used-car lot and the drive-in burger joint. 'Unlike the polish in MGM's extravagant A-production of *The Postman Always Rings Twice* or Fox's prestige Oscar contender *Laura*,' writes Sheri Chinen Biesen, 'Ulmer boils things down to their essence.'[84] Again this may be attributable to the meagreness of the production, to what Jacques

Rivette once called the 'spirit of poverty', which permeates nearly every aspect of Ulmer's film, and also to the 'grim, "un-American" fatalism' typical of this sub-species of noir.[85] As James Naremore notes, 'The flimsy sets reinforce the theme of social and cultural impoverishment, and the actors seem to belong to the same marginal world as the characters they play.'[86] Though Naremore is reluctant to adopt the term film gris, he agrees that there are distinctions to be made in terms of the political and social dimensions treated in films that are often lumped together under the banner of noir.

If there is a particular greyness to *Detour*, in the political sense, it is not merely visual. Rather, it is embedded in the narrative, where, as Polan points out, the irreconcilability between the 'haves' and the 'have-nots' is laid bare. All four principal characters are, on some level, engaged in the crass pursuit of material wealth: Sue ventures to make it big in Hollywood; Al hopes to ride that wave with her; Haskell has his heart set on the track at Santa Anita; and Vera, a bottom feeder of the worst sort, will 'take a swing at whatever comes along'. All four strike out, and each of their tragic stories helps to accentuate the cruelness of 40s America, thus conjuring a society that appears, in the film's harsh rendering, morally bankrupt. In the words of Andrew Britton, 'They are free agents in a world which privileges the material wellbeing of the atomized individual above all else and which unofficially encourages the most vicious, unprincipled and irresponsible forms of personal rapacity.'[87]

California dreamin'

According to Donald Lyons, '*Detour* gets the *Drang nach Californien* so redolent of the times', its idiomatic and geographic references corresponding to 'the cheap songs' of its jukebox. For Lyons, Ulmer's film may be seen not so much as an example of film gris, but of film asphalte, a road movie of the highest order. It is, in his estimation, 'the fullest expression of the mere road picture. . . . It is all there: sex as danger, life as a trap, road as taking you not just nowhere, but into nothingness.'[88] Yet, if *Detour* is to be considered a road movie, film

Al and Vera in LA

asphalte or otherwise, then we must recognise, as Michael Henry Wilson astutely points out, 'it is a road movie that couldn't afford roads, only strips of desert on a rear-projection screen'.[89] As the California dream of Al Roberts plays itself out, it becomes clear that he will never be safe and warm in LA. What he has instead is the decidedly cold backdrop, Coca-Cola sign and all, projected behind him and Vera as they drive through the city streets. According to Polan, *Detour* 'rewrites positive Los Angeles images to turn the California Dream into a nightmare'; the gloomy topography, in particular the desert, is not the common 'romantic space of discovery', often attributed to road film, but rather 'an empty, immaterial wasteland'.[90] In the words of Theodor Adorno, writing in the section of his *Minima Moralia* entitled '*Paysage*':

The shortcoming of the American landscape is not so much, as romantic illusion would have it, the absence of historical memories, as that it bears no traces of the human hand. This applies not only to the lack of arable land, the uncultivated woods often no higher than scrub, but above all to the roads. These are always inserted directly in the landscape, and the more impressively smooth and broad they are, the more unrelated and violent their gleaming track appears against its wild, overgrown surroundings.[91]

A mismatch for desert living

As Al makes his trek out west, the inhospitable nature of the desert, juxtaposed with the open road, is fully palpable on the screen, the sheer incompatibility between Al and his hostile environs highlighted with wrenching force.

Hollywood is, like the rest of the wasteland portrayed in Al's cross-country journey, a counterpart to the desert (Brecht's preferred metaphor), a place in which one can easily fall prey to greed, materialism, deception and scorching heat of all kinds. From the moment that Al arrives with Vera in Hollywood, the alienation sets in: Al notes in his voice-over narration that the distance between him and Sue is, paradoxically, greater now than when he began his journey; that he is imprisoned, stuck to Vera like 'Siamese twins', and none of the schemes she cooks up will ever allow him a way out. Hollywood is by no stretch of the imagination a Tinseltown. As Ulmer has it, there is no glamour, no glitz. In one of the most revealing scenes from *Detour* in which the California dream is shown to be anything but, Al and Vera leave behind their shady dealings at a used-car lot – after their aborted attempt to sell Haskell's car – and pull over at a drive-in for a little lunch and the announcement of Vera's final get-rich proposition. The drive-in serves as a reminder of Sue's harrowing descent from an aspiring starlet to a hash-slinger,

Car culture at the Los Angeles drive-in

and it quickly becomes the site of further ill-fated machinations (Vera's plot to have Al stand in for Haskell as heir to his father's fortune). The car culture of Los Angeles is at its most extreme, as the two actors remain firmly enclosed in Haskell's 'bus', the space that they share marked by the same extreme tension as in the squalid rooms they otherwise inhabit in their seemingly immovable condition of stalemate, waiting for death.

As Dana Polan has commented, the main characters in *Detour* resemble the Middle Americans in Hollywood portrayed in West's *The Day of the Locust*, and the words of West's narrator are similarly resonant: 'they had come here to die'.[92] Paradoxically, the memorandum from the Production Code Administration made a point of stating, 'If you decide to lay this story in Hollywood, it is important that [the actors] be so characterized as not to reflect discredit on the Motion Picture industry.' The 'discredit' that the actors reflect in *Detour* is not only a defamation of the film business (Sue's tragic fall) but of the American Dream as a whole, those industry-imposed happy endings that Al addresses in his sarcastic voice-over imagining what would happen if he and Vera fell in love. This is arguably the most subversive, overtly oppositional aspect of *Detour*: a full-frontal assault on Hollywood, its self-image, its strategies and practices.

Shadows of Weimar

Near the end of *Detour*, what is frequently taken for film noir
suddenly seems to get blended with the German *Kammerspielfilm*
(chamber play or domestic drama) tradition, as we enter into that
stifling, oxygen-deprived 'love nest' one final time.

Ulmer reintroduces us to the setting by framing it with curtains,
viewed through the window from the outside, giving the audience a
perspective that resembles that of a theatre stage. Al remarks, in his
voice-over, while he and Vera play a half-hearted game of cards,
that they were merely 'trying to kill time between newspaper
editions', and that this languishing state had become a 'death watch
for Vera' (waiting for news of Charles Haskell Sr's surrender to
pneumonia or, perhaps, for their own death). Here we get Al's
moralising discourse on avarice, a supplement to his earlier
commentary on money, and his attempt to talk Vera out of her go-
for-broke scheme. 'You're being a goon,' he barks at her.
'That's how people wind up behind the eight ball. Once they get a
few dollars they become greedy and want more.' On one level, Al's
commentary is a reflection of their individual situation of total
desperation, while on another it encapsulates a crude version of the

Detour as
Kammerspielfilm

Domestic drama in
extremis

The second framing of
Ulmer's chamber play

American capitalist spirit. The film suddenly becomes a morality
play, and its theatricality, something that was commonly
accentuated in cinema of the Weimar years, comes to the fore: Al
and Vera's explosive sparring choreographed as a domestic drama,
their protracted game of chicken in which each of them threatens to
turn the other in to the cops (with Vera 'drunk and crazy mad' and
Al facing the threat of a 'cute little gas chamber'), the stifling
quarters once more highlighted by the curtain frame of the chamber
play.

Critics have frequently drawn formal comparisons between German expressionism and film noir or between the so-called *Strassenfilm*, the street film, of classic Weimar cinema (e.g. Fritz Lang's celebrated film of 1922, *Dr Mabuse, the Gambler*, or Karl Grune's *The Street*, 1923) and film noir – thereby assuming a specific European lineage. Ulmer was certainly trained in Europe, and he apprenticed with some of the greatest stylists (Max Reinhardt, F. W. Murnau) of the era. Yet, unlike Lang, Ulmer never cut his teeth – at least not as a director, and not in any credited capacity – on either the expressionist or street films of his youth. Indeed, Ulmer was very eager to be associated with the great pictures of Weimar Germany, claiming at various points in his American career to have designed the sets for Robert Wiene's *Caligari* (1920) and Paul Wegener's *Golem* (1920), when he would have barely been a teenager; to have been assistant director and the brain behind the ground-breaking dolly shot in Murnau's *Der letzte Mann*; to have served as a designer on Lang's two *Nibelungen* films of 1924, on *Metropolis* (1927) and *M* – to which Lang later responded, unequivocally, 'Herr Ulmer never worked for me, neither as a film architect nor as a set designer, nor in any other capacity.'[93] Regardless of his dubious ties to these distinguished productions, Ulmer clearly identified with them and saw himself as part of their cultural and aesthetic mould.

When it comes to *Detour*, there are several stylistic gestures, subtle touches and self-avowed debts to Weimar cinema. The use of the oversized coffee mug, for instance, as the film shifts into flashback and the camera tracks in on Al's partially illuminated eyes, helps to heighten the oneiric quality of Al's story and, in doing so, uses a device that harks back to German expressionism and, more broadly, bears affinities in terms of design with Murnau.[94] Similarly, the shadow jazz players who emerge in Al's nocturnal dream of Sue bear strong resemblance to German films of the early 20s (in particular, Robison's *Schatten*). Ulmer himself remarks in his interview with Bogdanovich that he began his career in film as a cutter of silhouettes used for shadowy effect. In the same interview, Ulmer discusses *Detour* in relation to other Weimar-era films. He remarks of the plight of Al Roberts: 'He's so down on his luck that the girl who goes to the coast is the only person he can exist with sex-wise – *The Blue Angel* kind of thing.' Any serious connection – save, perhaps, for the magnetic, near-intoxicating attraction that Sue sparks in Al – between *Detour* and Sternberg's *Blue Angel* may be difficult to sustain. Yet, the fact that Ulmer still found himself, at the peak of his career, relying on the glories of Weimar cinema, glories with which he himself had little to do, to explain his own aesthetic choices is worth our attention. (Just a few years before shooting *Detour*, Ulmer had expressed his short-lived hope of remaking *The Blue Angel*, starring Veronica Lake.[95]) In the end, Ulmer took Goldsmith's material and infused it with a European sensibility, one shaped by the canon of classic Weimar cinema, avant-garde art, music and literature.

In terms of Ulmer's broader European training and intellectual background, critics have drawn comparisons, in style, sensibility and character, between *Detour* and such diverse literary and cultural luminaries as Gide, Freud, Sartre, Camus and Kafka. Writing in a programme note from a 1978 screening at the University of Texas, David Rodowick observes, 'In retrospect, *Detour* may be one of the great unrecognized works of the absurdist style, rivalling even Kafka in its determination to strip life of logic and stability.'[96] The film is certainly absurdist, insofar as the absurdist tradition denies the possibility of ever finding true meaning, which in the case of *Detour* is fundamental to the film's moral ambiguity and its characterisation of human futility in the face of the greater forces of fate. (According to Arthur Lyons, Al's famous line on fate and its ability to 'put a finger on you or me for no good reason at all' is 'not far from existentialist Albert Camus's contention that "at any street corner the absurd may strike a man in the face." '[97]) Without making too much of Ulmer's background in German and European letters, it is perhaps possible to regard *Detour* as the work of a director who was quite indebted – and indeed fashioned himself as someone with a profound intellectual indebtedness – to the European avant-garde. Born as he was into the Habsburg Empire of the *fin de siècle*, Ulmer was surely aware of Kafka and Freud, of Musil, Schnitzler and Karl Kraus. More specifically, Kafka's acute distrust of authority, his ruminations on guilt and more generally on the moral impoverishment of humanity may well have resonated powerfully with the director.

With respect to Sartre, who was very much the rage around the time of *Detour*'s release and around the time that French critics were beginning to think of American cinema of the 40s in terms of noir, the affinities are quite palpable. In the words of one critic,

Detour can ultimately seem not that removed from the despairing existential effort of a Sartre in *Huis clos* (aptly translated as 'No exit'): certainly, the long sequence in which a desperate Al and an ever more shrill Vera spar bitterly in a hotel room distinguished only by its barrenness seems an apt visualization of Sartre's dictum that 'Hell is other people.'[98]

Sartre's play, which debuted the year before Ulmer's film, emerged from the same cultural ferment of wartime misery. Like Al and Vera, the players in *No Exit* are made to suffer from the condition of their abject confinement, from the hellish interrogation of each other's human standing.

There is little doubt that packed into the mere sixty-eight minutes of screen time is a diverse amalgamation of stylistic currents, aesthetic concerns and cultural allusions, many of them with notable antecedents within the vast sweep of European ideas. In Grissemann's critical account,

one could call *Detour* a film under the influence (or, more simply, expressionist cinema): The damaged sense of perception from which all three main figures suffer (the pill-dependent Haskell, the alcoholic Vera, the traumatized Al) appears to give the film its essential form.[99]

6 Detour Redux

'Remakes are always high risk,' remarks Foster Hirsch in his *Detours and Lost Highways: A Map of Neo-Noir*:

Unavoidably, they are read against the grain of the original works, and because they confront the widespread cultural belief that the first of any form is the purest version, they are stamped with what amounts to, in effect, a primal curse.[100]

If, as some have claimed, Ulmer's *Detour* is to be regarded a film maudit, then any attempt at a remake must be doubly 'maudit'. That dim prospect did not, however, keep others (even Ulmer himself) from taking a stab at reworking the film – whether by setting it in a different time and place, attempting to replicate the original with even greater fidelity to Goldsmith's story or offering a stylistic homage to the original – in the many years since its release. For different reasons at differing moments in time, the urge to rethink Ulmer's film has spawned several productions, some of them fully executed, others left merely to collect dust. While Hirsch's cautionary words point to the inherent risks of the remake genre per se, some of the attempts at redoing *Detour* lie far beyond the genre's basic parameters.

The Loser

In 1968, several years after he had completed what would be his last picture, the claustrophobic war film *Sette contro la morte* (*The Cavern*, 1964), a German–Italian co-production shot in the mountains of Yugoslavia, Ulmer decided to return one final time to the story of *Detour*. One of the very few press reviews of *The Cavern* noted how director Ulmer 'perks up' the pace toward the end, but

otherwise judged the film 'small, respectable and forgettable'.[101]
There can be little doubt that Ulmer did not wish to go down in
history with that epitaph attached to his name. By that point, after a
generally inauspicious stretch of directing in Europe, from *I pirati di
Capri* (*Pirates of Capri*, 1949) and *Muchachas de Bagdad* (*Babes in
Bagdad*, 1952) through *L'Atlandide* (*Journey beneath the Desert*,
1961), films that often went entirely unnoticed – some for good
reason – the original sparkle of *Detour* began to regain some of its
lustre on his résumé of lifetime achievements. Although there were
other projects in the works (a few freelance television production
assignments with the *Doris Day Show*), here was a chance to revisit a
project that had once meant, and indeed, as his 1970 interview with
Peter Bogdanovich surely attests ('the idea to get involved on that
road of Fate – where he's an absolute loser – fascinated me'),
continued to mean an enormous amount to the director.

The screenplay he produced, entitled 'The Loser' and registered
with the Screen Writers Guild in 1969, opens in Greenwich Village of
the present, with crowds of hippies and hookers pouring out onto
MacDougal Street, and ends in a San Francisco phone booth where
our hero, a young rock musician who slogs through a similarly
doomed cross-country journey, is picked up by the cops for
murder.[102] The hero, Steve Bryan, is of course a late-60s rendition of
Al Roberts: 'educated at the Julliard School', he is 'quite ordinary
looking except for his hair which is cut in the mod style'. Steve plays
guitar in a band called The Ghouls at a down-and-out rock club
called Concrete Canyon – with go-go dancers in cages, among them
Steve's girl, Sandy Lewis, and walls decorated with psychedelic
posters and a 'highly stylized quasi-saintlike picture of Bob Dylan'.
Also in the club, alongside the junkies and teeny-boppers, prostitutes
turn tricks and a charismatic pimp named Robert E. Lee (breathing
new life into the moniker once attached to the famous Confederate
general) controls the show. Owing to a cold-hearted scheme by
Robert E., who has Steve's girl in his grip, Sandy gets sent out ('sold')
to a friend who owns a big joint in San Francisco. Ulmer has the

transaction take place inside the pimp's apartment, a seedy gathering spot ('There must be an old detour leading through my pad'), where Robert E. is serviced by one of his girls.

Compared to the pimp, Steve is positively upstanding, of a different class altogether, his apartment decorated with prints by Picasso and home to a Steinway grand piano. He has plans to marry Sandy, whom he first met at a peace demonstration. Yet like Sue Harvey, Sandy rebuffs his offer and declares things over between them. In her trite formulation: 'Some guys win and some guys lose. Well, you're a loser baby.' Like Al, Steve ends up hawking his possessions and heading off on a westward trek to reunite with a woman he will never reach and who, we are given to believe, wouldn't want him there anyway (Sandy's callousness matches Goldsmith's characterisation of Sue more closely than the pared-down film version). As fate would have it – no major surprise here – somewhere outside Oklahoma City Steve hops into a brand-new 1969 Cadillac convertible driven by a brash, pill-popping blowhard named Bob Simmons, a man whose left hand bears 'three ugly, new gashes'. The rest of the story, as we might expect, follows the basic arc of Goldsmith's screenplay, with a few updates and embellishments: Bob tells Steve of his heroic tussle with Chris Logan ('a helluva good-looking bitch') and passes out from his pills and liquor, never to wake up again; Steve takes the wheel, enjoys an erotic fantasy of Sandy (The Ghouls suddenly emanating from the car radio) before, yes, in a rainstorm, he pulls over, tries in vain to wake Bob up, opens his door and finds Bob lying on a pile of rocks next to the road. At the next gas station, Chris climbs into the car, demands to know what happened with Bob and naturally exploits her information to hold Steve hostage ('Your trouble is my fortune'). Finally, after many heated arguments and some angry sex in between, Chris gets the same telephone treatment as Vera, while Steve's last phone call, placed right before getting nabbed by the cops, reveals that Sandy has run off with another man.[103] Without the snappy prose of Martin Goldsmith, who by then had earned an Oscar nomination for his story adapted in Richard Fleischer's *The Narrow Margin* (1952), Ulmer's screenplay does not quite have the same verve; rather, its main appeal is as a document of its time and of its author.

Although it is not entirely clear where Ulmer intended to shop the script, in retrospect its commercial viability does not appear to have been particularly robust. Many of his champions have argued that he self-consciously snubbed Hollywood and the big studio dynasties, preferring instead to work independently, but that assertion is only a half-truth. There is no question that he enjoyed the professional freedom accorded to him at PRC, where he was not merely one of their most appreciated directors but, for all intents and purposes, had the leeway of a head of production. In his personal correspondence, however, an unabashed desire to work within the studio system and finally to receive the credit he deserved crops up periodically. In the summer of 1941, just a year before he began his tenure at PRC, Ulmer writes to his wife Shirley of his meeting at Paramount. The letter, dated 1 July and printed on stationery from the Hollywood Plaza Hotel, strikes a decidedly optimistic note:

The prayer has worked. Sweetest I am so excited I hardly can hold the pen in my hand. I just returned from Paramount. Sherle, they have not forgotten. Sherle, I am as good as signed with Paramount. Producer – director – good God! Sweets we are home again and on the way.[104]

These words, which almost could be uttered by Al Roberts, when he is fleetingly in a giddy state before heading off to Hollywood to meet Sue, do not reflect the view of a man who turned his back on the studios.

One of the few English-language profiles devoted to Ulmer during his lifetime was published in *The New York Times* in 1966 under the apt title 'How to be a Loner in Hollywood'. The writer, Peter Bart, suggests that Ulmer managed throughout his career to distinguish himself, almost defiantly, as 'the professional loner' from the 'proficient organization men' who dominated the industry. In the same article, Ulmer is quoted comparing the fate of the director in Europe versus America: 'In Europe, no one can be a "loner," an outsider in his own profession. There are always eager young film-makers who are studying your films and who regard you as their teacher. But here things are different.'[105] It was around this same time that he was thinking up the screenplay for his remake – one that rather consciously caters to the younger generation, a generation that might be more inclined to appreciate his work – whose alternative title was, quite fittingly, 'The Loner'. There remained in Ulmer a profound identification with the plight of the hero, his inability to follow the straight and narrow, his unrecognised talent and dedication, his seemingly innate ability to fall into life's traps and be led astray.

Reliving Detour

Ulmer was not the only one whose life and career bore personal affinities with the film he made in 1945. In one of the more bizarre cases of life imitating art, on the evening of 1 April 1965, Tom Neal, by then working as a gardener in Palm Springs, walked into the Tyrol, an Alpine restaurant in the neighbouring town of Idyllwild, where he was a regular, and announced to the owners that he had killed his wife. Neal had a streak of violence in his past. His well-hyped brawl with Franchot Tone over blonde bombshell Barbara Payton, a future lead in Ulmer's *Murder is My Beat* (1955), made major headlines in 1951: the *Los Angeles Herald Express* announced in extra-large, bold-face type, 'Tom Neal Knocks Out Tone In Love Fist Fight'.[106] Despite Neal's sensationalised past, often presented as his given reason for retreating to the desert, the owners of the Tyrol expressed incredulity at what he had to say that night. 'This is not an April Fool's joke,' Neal insisted, 'it's true.'

Early the next morning, the police entered Neal's home and found Gail Neal (née Kloke) dead on the couch, shot in the head with a .45 automatic. The story behind her murder, as it seeped into the courtroom later that autumn, included Gail's rumoured plans for divorce and, from Tom's side, allegations of her multiple affairs and threats to kill him. For weeks on end, the drama maintained a tawdry air of celebrity, Barbara Payton consistently seated among the spectators, and all eyes focused on Tom Neal. Arthur Lyons claims that in the courtroom Neal managed to achieve 'what had escaped him in his film career – top billing'.[107] Most astounding was Neal's defence: a mere accident, 'the gun went off' (the pathologist who conducted the autopsy called his account 'unlikely', but Neal's version held up before the jury). He was charged with involuntary manslaughter, and served six years of a maximum fifteen-year sentence. After his early release from prison, it was only a matter of months before he himself was found dead, the victim of heart failure, discovered in his Hollywood apartment by his son, Tom Jr.

In yet another ironic twist of fate, Tom Neal Jr would go on to play his father's role of Al Roberts in the 1992 remake of *Detour* by director Wade Williams. An avid collector and sometimes producer of horror, sci-fi and cult movies, Williams took great pains to recreate Ulmer's film – tracking down the same car he had used, a 1941 Lincoln convertible, and doing all that he could to include even the smallest details in his rendition – while at the same time resuscitating parts of Goldsmith's script that had originally wound up in the dustbin. It's hard to imagine anyone other than a hardcore *Detour* cult fan making this film; it's equally hard to imagine anyone other than a hardcore *Detour* cult fan watching it. The peculiar nature of Williams's venture seems to presuppose prior exposure to Ulmer's *Detour* on the part of the audience. Who else could possibly understand what Williams's fanatically reconstructed bits are all about? As Michael Atkinson puts it, 'seeing it without a thorough foreknowledge of the original movie would be a bit like a New Guinea tribesman tripping through Madame Tussaud's'.[108]

Williams sets the film in 1942 and uses various cues to let the audience know the mood he is seeking to convey. Compared to the original, the backdrop of the war is considerably more apparent, with Vera at one point asking Al why he's not in uniform. There are also a couple of early (Brecht-inspired?) inter-titles offering a shorthand gloss, in the spirit of Goldsmith's dark cynicism, on the ugly underbelly of 40s Hollywood, with slogans like 'Mecca of broken promises and unfulfilled dreams' and 'One of the foulest traps imaginable'. An untested actor, Tom Neal Jr essentially plays his father playing Al Roberts, and Lea Lavish, also untested, plays Ann Savage playing Vera, both of their performances more impersonations than independent roles. Neal Jr clogs up several of his voice-over lines with audible nasal congestion. Lavish, on the other hand, manages on occasion to hit the intonation of Ann Savage (for instance, when she snarls, 'We're out of liquor, Roberts!'), while her accompanying gestures and facial expressions are generally less convincing. A question that David Thomson raises in reference to the film's original players seems equally apt here: 'were these actors, hoping for careers, or derelicts resolved to treat the idea of a movie with contempt?'[109] Though Williams makes an effort to return the upper hand to Goldsmith, giving Sue (Erin McGrane) her own voice-over account and allowing Al to elude the cops in the end,[110] he also ends up adding several jarring lines of dialogue (e.g. 'That's fate, Roberts, life takes a little detour every now and then'), and a new theme song entitled 'Careless' that has the ring of a schmaltzy Barry Manilow number.

As Foster Hirsch puts it, recalling Atkinson's allusion to Madame Tussaud's, 'If the primary aim is simply to duplicate or recapture, the remake can be no more than a waxworks simulation.'[111] In this case, the heavily choreographed, obsessively studied simulation has a particularly creepy, at times even sleazy air to it – German critic Bert Rebhandel has suggested, in a slightly polemical vein, 'The new *Detour* is the work of an epigone in whose hands the film's direction makes every scene appear as if it were a leftover from a porno shoot.'[112] That may be unduly harsh, given the impossible task of remaking a film like *Detour*. Still, we might agree, if only playfully, that some of the more lurid moments of Williams's film evoke a kind of retro skin flick without the skin.

Reinhabiting Detour

Williams was certainly not the first, nor the last, to revisit Ulmer's *Detour*. Belgian-born director Carl Colpaert offered his on-the-road homage in *Delusion* (1991), and the Coen brothers gave an understated, spiritual nod to Al Roberts in their portrayal of barber Ed Crane in *The Man Who Wasn't There* (2000). Somewhat more substantially, Greil Marcus has recently made a powerful argument for interpreting David Lynch's *Lost Highway* (1997) not as a 'rewrite' or 'remake' of *Detour*, but as a kind of 'reinhabiting' of the film. According to Marcus, 'Lynch's movie emerges from Ulmer's, inside out, just as, when *Lost Highway* plays, Ulmer's movie emerges from Lynch's, flattening it, exposing its surfaces, linking one broken line down the middle of a road to another.'[113]

The parallels between the two films begin with those lines of the open road, that is, with the two credit sequences that set the films in motion: the reverse tracking shot in *Detour* and an accelerated, seemingly handheld track forward, gripping the nocturnal road, in *Lost Highway*. What follows are more subtle links in character and motif. For instance, the crazed shots of Fred Madison (Bill Pullman) playing a charged free-jazz number on his sax at the Luna Lounge may recall the feverish, frustrated medley that Al Roberts plays at the Break O'Dawn. Or, in what Marcus considers to be possibly the only overt reference to *Detour* in the film, Pete Dayton (Balthazar Getty), at that point assuming the role of Fred Madison, hears Fred's compulsive improvisation playing on the radio and rushes to turn it off, a scene that might recall both Al's early jukebox outburst in the Nevada diner and his later aversion, when cooped up with Vera in LA, to the off-screen saxophone player – all three instances unwanted reminders of a tortured past. Still later, when Pete asks femme fatale Alice Wakefield (Patricia Arquette) 'Why me, Alice?', there is a faint echo in the lyrics to 'I Can't Believe that You're in Love with Me'.

Moreover, according to Marcus, there is the impotence of both Al Roberts and Fred Madison, and the strange doubling that each of them undergoes with Haskell and Dayton, respectively. Then, too, there is Vera. 'Except for the sex scene in the desert,' writes Marcus, 'which in 1945 could only have been shot for a porn movie, Patricia Arquette's Alice walks in the footsteps of Ann Savage's Vera, and falls behind.'[114] Lynch can't resist toying with the audience's voyeuristic impulses, making it sometimes appear that the film's co-stars are Arquette's breasts rather than Arquette herself; had Ulmer been afforded the chance to cast Ann Savage in as explicit a role as Alice, well, he too might have leaped at the opportunity (his 1969 screenplay is brimming with scenes of unbridled sex and voyeurism that would have been unthinkable a quarter-century earlier and that make his 1958 low-budget nudie *The Naked Venus* seem like Disney).

By the time we finally enter the Lost Highway Hotel, near the close of the film, everything has turned in on itself. Like *Detour*, Lynch's film doesn't take place in a real location, but rather in the hotels of the mind, whose parlours we sometimes enter when our subconscious trains of thought lead us down dark alleyways. What we don't realise until the end of *Lost Highway* is that Fred Madison is the one tearing down that same strip of nocturnal highway we encounter in the first seconds of the film, trying to escape the cops – or, perhaps, merely to escape the cops in his mind (as Al Roberts puts it, soon after he resumes his trek on the open highway following Haskell's death, 'I kept imagining I was being followed, that I could hear sirens back in the distance'). From the credit sequence onward, in both films the endless desolate highway – flitting by at an uncontrollable speed – serves as a poignant leitmotif for the nightmarish road that each protagonist will travel and in whose face each will prove utterly powerless.

Postscript: Alone in the Dark

Not altogether different from other films with the capacity to elicit a visceral response in the viewer (Lang's *M*, Hitchcock's *Vertigo*, 1958, Lynch's *Blue Velvet*, 1986, *et al.*), *Detour* is, by many accounts, the kind of picture that burrows itself deeply and indefinitely into the viewer's nervous system. It can leave you unsettled, beside yourself or perhaps merely with a gnawing urge to jump in a shower and scrub off the grime that seems to have accumulated during Al's inexorable decline. *Detour* is, as some have claimed, 'an exercise in sustained perversity' and the kind of experiment in celluloid that appears as if it emerged from its canisters 'dripping with disgust'.[115] Commentators frequently feel compelled to address the nature of their subjective viewing experience of the film in their assessment.

Consider, for instance, the reflections of film curator Lizzie Francke: 'There are some moments in a girl's cinema-going career that she'll never forget. She is taken by surprise in the darkness as some film stands out and makes you want to know a little more.' Francke goes on to recall her first viewing of *Detour*, sometime in the 80s, at London's Scala cinema at King's Cross, a place that 'smelt like a pub and rumbled every time a Tube train went by'. As she sat in the dark, something happened; what transpired on the screen, and the style in which it was presented, left a stark imprint on her. 'The fog, the darkness,' she writes, 'the dingy motel room walls, the manic consumptive moll who diverts him on his way. I felt it all in the half-empty Scala.'[116]

In a slight variation on Francke's remarks, American poet John Ashbery notes in his recent vignette on the picture, '*Detour* is an unpleasant movie that somehow lodges in the memory and invites repeated viewings.' For Ashbery, who cannot put his finger on the single element that brings about this effect – it may be the 'threadbare sets' or the 'low-rent cast' or even the 'airless backdrops' – the film ultimately evokes 'lost afternoons in the third-run movie palaces of my youth'.[117] For me, and I presume for others as well, *Detour* has its own place of origin, its own register of memories. I first saw the picture, a shoddy, patched-up 16mm print, as a graduate student in Berkeley in the 90s. Despite the grainy, low-quality image – or, perhaps, because of its astonishing rawness and its brazenly unpolished air – the film grabbed a hold of me and never seems to have let go. A good ten years later, at a screening in Vienna's Film Museum, I sat alone in the dark on one of the auditorium's notoriously uncomfortable wooden seats, watching with rapt attention all sixty-eight minutes of the restored, surprisingly spotless 35mm print. This, of course, was for me the ultimate viewing experience – right in the heart of the city that the director once called home, with all of its former grandeur, and yet still gritting my teeth, denied the very possibility of ever being lulled into some kind of blissful Hollywood epic dream. No, *Detour* will never be that picture.

Notes

1 The term 'lemonade-stand budget'
derives from Michael Atkinson's
insightful analysis of *Detour* and its 1992
remake by Wade Williams, 'Noir and
Away', *Bright Lights*, no. 15 (Winter
1995), p. 30.
2 See Wade Williams's account in 'Edgar
Ulmer's Dark Excursion into the
Nightmare World of Fatal Irony . . .',
Filmfax, no. 11 (July 1988), pp. 22–5.
His discussion of Goldsmith, citing a
conversation with the novelist, takes
place on p. 24. A film collector and
Ulmer enthusiast, Williams holds the
rights on the 2000 DVD release of *Detour*
by Image Entertainment. In 1992, his
obsessively faithful remake of the film,
including scenes from Goldsmith's
script that were cut from Ulmer's
production, was released. An unsigned
profile of Goldsmith is also contained in
the appended materials to the reprint
of his complete script in *Scenario*, vol. 3
no. 2 (Summer 1997), p. 179.
3 Arthur Lyons, *Death on the Cheap: The
Lost B Movies of Film Noir* (New York: Da
Capo, 2000), p. 48. In his incisive
reading of Ulmer's *Detour* and David
Lynch's *Lost Highway*, Greil Marcus has
suggested that PRC almost sounds like
'a front for organized crime'. See his
'American Berserk: Bill Pullman's Face',
in *The Shape of Things to Come: Prophecy
and the American Voice* (New York:
Farrar, Straus and Giroux, 2006), p. 130.
See also Richard Combs, 'Edgar G.
Ulmer and PRC: A Detour down Poverty
Row', *Monthly Film Bulletin*, vol. 49
no. 582 (July 1982), p. 152; and Wheeler
Dixon (ed.), *Producers Releasing
Corporation: A Comprehensive*
Filmography and History (Jefferson, NC:
McFarland, 1986).
4 Charles Flynn and Todd McCarthy,
'The Economic Imperative: Why was the
B Movie Necessary?', in McCarthy and
Flynn (eds), *Kings of the Bs: Working
within the Hollywood System* (New York:
E. P. Dutton & Co., 1975), pp. 13–43, here
p. 13. On PRC, see Dixon, *Producers
Releasing Corporation*.
5 Edwin Schallert, 'Super Man Hunt Will
Spark "War Criminals"', *Los Angeles
Times*, 20 October 1944. Schallert notes
further that Martin Mooney will
supervise the project and that 'Tom
Neal is being sought for the lead'.
There is no mention of Edgar G. Ulmer.
6 In Eddie Muller's account, the ex-
boxer and infamous womaniser Neal
made his on-set acquaintance with
Savage in an especially gruff fashion:
'Swaggering through the costumed
revellers, he came up behind her,
clutched Ann in an embrace, and
started tonguing her ear. "I belted him
in the jaw," Ann says. The set fell silent.
"Nobody was going to play me cheap.
Certainly not some muscle-headed
macho man, showing off for his
friends."' *Dark City Dames: The Wicked
Women of Film Noir* (New York:
HarperCollins, 2001), p. 151.
7 Williams, 'Edgar Ulmer's Dark
Excursion', p. 24. See also Stefan
Grissemann's sketch of the transaction
in *Mann im Schatten: Der Filmemacher
Edgar G. Ulmer* (Vienna: Zsolnay, 2003),
p. 217.
8 Allegedly, Goldsmith made this (i.e.
that he write his own screenplay) a
condition of the sale. See the brief

profile appended to his reprinted script in *Scenario*, p. 179. This unusual move was picked up by contemporary reviewers, with Jim Henaghan of the *Hollywood Reporter* commenting, 'He [Martin Mooney] is to be congratulated for breaking the rules to the extent of permitting the author to write his own screen story.' See his 'Detour', *Hollywood Reporter*, 29 October 1945.

9 John Belton gives a thorough elaboration of the term, and its application to Ulmer, in his chapter on Ulmer in Jean-Pierre Coursodon's *American Directors*, vol. 1 (New York: McGraw-Hill, 1983), p. 340. Luc Moullet's reappraisal of Ulmer appears in *Cahiers du cinéma*, no. 58 (April 1956), pp. 55–7.

10 Andrew Sarris, *The American Cinema* (New York: Dutton, 1968), p. 143. The subsequent remark comes from his 'Beatitudes of B Pictures', in McCarthy and Flynn, *Kings of the Bs*, p. 52.

11 See Peter Bogdanovich, 'Edgar G. Ulmer: An Interview', *Film Culture*, nos. 58–60 (1974), reprinted in *Who the Devil Made It: Conversations with Legendary Film Directors* (New York: Ballantine, 1998), pp. 558–604; Myron Meisel, 'Edgar G. Ulmer: The Primacy of the Visual', in McCarthy and Flynn, *Kings of the Bs*, pp. 147–52, here p. 151; and John Belton, *Howard Hawks, Frank Borzage, Edgar G. Ulmer* (New York: A. S. Barnes & Co., 1974), p. 162.

12 Kevin Thomas, 'UCLA Focuses on "The King of the B's"', *Los Angeles Times*, 6 October 1983. Thomas, who calls *Detour* 'a riveting study of guilt and paranoia', asserts further, 'For the past 20 years the reputation of Ulmer, widely crowned the King of the Bs, has grown steadily as a virtuoso stylist who could turn out highly personal films in any genre on minuscule budgets.'

13 Deborah Caulfield, 'So What Ever Happened to Bad Girl Ann Savage?', *Los Angeles Times*, 17 February 1985. See also Eddie Muller's account of Savage's return, in *Dark City Dames*, pp. 274–7.

14 Mike Spies, 'Edgar G. Who?', *Houston Chronicle*, 5 March 1984.

15 Scott Cain, 'Month of Screenings Honors Career of "King of the B's"', *Atlanta Constitution*, 31 March 1986.

16 Roger Ebert, '*Detour* (1945)', *Chicago Sun-Times*, 7 June 1998.

17 Kent Jones, '*Detour* (VI)', *LIT*, no. 13 (Autumn 2007), p. 140. The commentary by Martin Scorsese comes from the section 'The Director as Smuggler' in *A Personal Journey with Martin Scorsese through American Movies* (1995).

18 All citations from Goldsmith's novel are taken from the original edition, *Detour: An Extraordinary Tale* (New York: Macaulay, 1939). Citations from Goldsmith's screenplay come from the reprint in *Scenario*, pp. 133–78. All citations from Ulmer's film are from the 2000 DVD release by Image Entertainment.

19 Edgar G. Ulmer, 'The Director's Responsibility', unsourced document contained in The Edgar G. Ulmer Collection, Margaret Herrick Library, Academy of Motion Picture Arts and Sciences, Beverly Hills, CA.

20 Robert Polito, 'Some Detours to *Detour*', *LIT*, no. 13 (Autumn 2007), p. 148. Polito also serves as editor of the issue's dossier of tributes and reconsiderations, 'Detour: A Symposium on Edgar Ulmer's 1945 PRC Film Noir', with contributions by Greil Marcus, A. J. Albany, Geoffrey O'Brien, John Ashbery, Guy Maddin, Kent Jones and Arianné Ulmer Cipes.

21 In his account, Greil Marcus sees the basic distinguishing features of Haskell and Roberts as nearly identical. He notes of their initial encounter, when Haskell stops to give Al a lift: 'As the car pulls out, Ulmer, shooting from behind, shows the two men as doubles: they're the same size, their suits are the same shade, even their hats are blocked in the same way.' See Marcus, *The Shape of Things to Come*, p. 133. The point Marcus makes is indeed compelling, though the particular scene he refers to is shot from a good distance, making the finer nuances of the individual characters even less detectable.

22 Bogdanovich, *Who the Devil Made It*, p. 558. Commenting in 1985 on the resurgence of interest in *Detour*, Ann Savage attributes the success solely to Ulmer: 'Without his direction, *Detour* would have been just another B.' Cited in Caulfield, 'So What Ever Happened to Bad Girl Ann Savage?'. Savage has claimed elsewhere, in an interview of 1992, 'I must give Martin Goldsmith credit. . . . It was all there in the script.' See A. G., 'Auteur Detour', *Scenario*, vol. 3 no. 2 (Summer 1997), p. 181.

23 Meisel, 'The Primacy of the Visual', p. 149. John Belton similarly notes how Ulmer was 'locked into a frustrating cycle of "B" pictures'. See his contribution to Coursodon's *American Directors*, p. 346.

24 See Richard Schickel, *Double Indemnity* (London: British Film Institute, 1992), p. 63.

25 See *Edgar G. Ulmer: Man Off-Screen* (2004), directed by Michael Palm, released on DVD from KINO International in 2006. Earlier in the same film, B-movie specialist Gregory Mank suggests that Ulmer had 'to take a rat and make Thanksgiving dinner out of it'. In his recent essay on *Detour*, Kent Jones notes that the more polemical auteurists of the 50s and 60s helped cook up 'the heroic scenario of the director with everything against him taking a sow's ear and making a silk purse out of it'. See 'Detour (VI)', p. 140.

26 Unpublished interview with Stefan Grissemann, Sherman Oaks, CA, 2 July 2001. In his interview with Bogdanovich, Ulmer explains his technique the same way: 'I shot my master scene, but left for the last day the close-ups.'

27 Tim Pulleine, '16mm/Detour (1945)', *Films and Filming*, no. 335 (August 1982), p. 37.

28 Eddie Muller, *Dark City: The Lost World of Film Noir* (New York: St Martin's Griffin, 1998), p. 178.

29 Sheri Chinen Biesen, *Blackout: World War II and the Origins of Film Noir* (Baltimore: Johns Hopkins University Press, 2005), p. 165. Gregory Mank's comment comes from Michael Palm's Ulmer documentary.

30 Grissemann, *Mann im Schatten*, p. 221.

31 Unpublished interview with the author, Bonita, CA, 16 December 2001.

32 William K. Everson, 'Introduction: Remembering PRC', in Dixon, *Producers Releasing Corporation*, p. 2.

33 Bogdanovich, *Who the Devil Made It*, p. 558.

34 Ulmer's daughter, Arianné Ulmer Cipes, points this out in an interview in 2007. See her '*Detour* (VII): Q&A', *LIT*, no. 13 (Autumn 2007), p. 143.

35 Ann Savage notes, in her interview with Michael Henry Wilson, 'I wouldn't be a bit surprised if Edgar didn't do that on purpose . . . Maybe his sense of humour, or something like that.' Unpublished interview with Michael Henry Wilson, Los Angeles, CA, 6 May 1996.

36 Andrew Britton, 'Detour', in Ian Cameron (ed.), *The Book of Film Noir* (New York: Continuum, 1993), p. 177.

37 Unpublished interview with Michael Henry Wilson, 6 May 1996.

38 James Naremore, *More than Night: Film Noir and its Contexts* (Berkeley: University of California Press, 1998), p. 149. As director Guy Maddin has observed: 'I feel even Bette Davis would be cautious in the presence of Vera – perhaps the only woman who could scare all the raging nightmares of Pandora's box into her own carry-on luggage, where they would be compelled to fold themselves up and lie obediently with her nighties and toiletries.' See his '*Detour* (V)', *LIT*, no. 13 (Autumn 2007), p. 139.

39 Marcus, *The Shape of Things to Come*, p. 135. Eddie Muller gives Savage's account of Ulmer's coaching ('Edgar snapped his fingers: *Faster! Faster! Pick up the Pace!*') in *Dark City Dames*, p. 161. He also quotes from a contemporary review of the film, from a publication in Providence, Rhode Island: 'The job Ann Savage does in *Detour*, a little melodrama from PRC, is nothing short of astounding. Here is a girl whose stock and trade heretofore has been to serve as animated blond pompadour and to lend her pretty face and lissom figure to the making of cheesecake stills. And yet, as Vera, she plays a thoroughly evil and scheming female in a style comparable only, to the best of my recollection, to Bette Davis's performance in *Of Human Bondage*' (p. 165).

40 See Chinen Biesen, *Blackout*, pp.165–6.

41 Memo of 1 November 1944, Joseph I. Breen to Martin Mooney, contained in the Margaret Herrick Library, Academy of Motion Picture Arts and Sciences, Beverly Hills, CA. All citations to the memo are taken from this document.

42 Unpublished interview with Michael Henry Wilson, 6 May 1996.

43 See Polito, 'Some Detours to *Detour*', p. 152. In his new biography of Otto Preminger, Foster Hirsch notes that 'Sophisticated Lady' was initially slated for use as the theme song in *Laura* (1944) until David Raskin scored his own original 'Laura' theme. See *Otto Preminger: The Man Who Would be King* (New York: Knopf, 2007), pp. 106–7.

44 See Caryl Flinn, *Strains of Utopia: Gender, Nostalgia, and Hollywood Film Music* (Princeton: Princeton University Press, 1992), p. 126.

45 Jim Henaghan, 'Detour', *Hollywood Reporter*, 29 October 1945.

46 'Detour', *Daily Variety*, 29 October 1945; 'Detour', *Film Daily*, 1 March 1946. A review by Mandel Herbstman, in the

Motion Picture Herald (10 November 1945), called *Detour* an 'adroit, albeit unpretentious production', while giving it a rating of 'fair'. In the UK, where the film's release appears to have been delayed for nearly a year, the reviewer for the *Monthly Film Bulletin* offers a blistering critique: 'This very poor story has little to commend it. It tries the unusual by interspersing dialogue with commentary in the form of Al talking to himself, and fails. The direction is as poor as the story. The only bright spot is Ann Savage's performance as Vera, which she does so well that she really leaves a taste of complete revulsion in the mouth.' See P. T., 'Detour', *Monthly Film Bulletin*, vol. 13 no. 154 (October 1946), p. 137.

47 '*Detour* Tears Emotions', *Los Angeles Times*, 30 October 1945.

48 Tania Modleski, 'Film Theory's Detour', *Screen*, vol. 23 no. 5 (November–December 1982), p. 75.

49 Ibid.

50 In an interview in 2007, Arianné Ulmer Cipes gives a more personal reading of the film noting her father's attraction to the idea of the 'dominant manipulative woman who pushes the weak self-destructive male'. As she explains it, 'Ulmer's mother was a highly controlling difficult woman (according to the whole family). He was always working through his ambivalence and attraction to this type of female.' See her 'Detour (VII): Q&A', p. 143. By contrast, Andrew Britton sees Ulmer's portrayal of women in *Detour* as a means of highlighting a culture that 'is permeated by inequalities of sexual power, and that Sue and Vera are oppressed as women'. See Britton, 'Detour', p. 178.

51 Britton, 'Detour', p. 174.

52 John Belton, 'Film Noir's Knights of the Road', *Bright Lights*, no. 12 (Spring 1994), p. 14.

53 Britton, 'Detour', p. 174. As Erik Ulman has commented, 'Al may indeed be a victim of fate, but he hardly cuts his losses: his criminating assumption of Haskell's identity, his immediate and craven acquiescence to the malevolent Vera's plans, his diffidence about contacting Sue, and his excessively effective manner of silencing Vera obliterate any purported innocence.' See Ulman, 'Edgar G. Ulmer', *Senses of Cinema* (January–February 2003), <www.sensesofcinema.com/contents/directors/03/ulmer.html>, accessed 3 March 2003.

54 Britton, 'Detour', p. 180.

55 Cited in Deborah Lazaroff Alpi, *Robert Siodmak* (Jefferson, NC: McFarland, 1998), p. 20. Ulmer's reputation as a teller of tall tales was further immortalised in a 1990 article on apocryphal Hollywood stories. See Dale Thomajan, 'Ready When You Are, Mr Ulmer', *Film Comment*, vol. 26 no. 3 (March–April 1990), pp. 67–8.

56 Charles Tesson, 'Hollywood ou mourir', *Cahiers du cinéma*, vol. 436 (October 1990), cited in Peter Nau, 'Das Geheimnis der Form in den Filmen Edgar G. Ulmers', in Christian Cargnelli and Michael Omasta (eds), *Aufbruch ins Ungewisse: Österreichische Filmschaffende in der Emigration vor 1945* (Vienna: Wespennest, 1993), p. 131.

57 Alexander Horwath, 'Das Shining: *Strange Illusion* von Edgar G. Ulmer (1945)', in Christian Cargnelli and Michael Omasta (eds), *Schatten. Exil: Europäische Emigranten im Film Noir* (Vienna: PVS, 1997), p. 299.
58 On the further symbolic potential of Al's journey, read through a musical lens, see Ulman, 'Edgar G. Ulmer'.
59 Edward Said, 'Reflections on Exile', *Granta*, no. 13 (Autumn 1984), pp. 159–72, reprinted in Marc Robinson (ed.), *Altogether Elsewhere: Writers on Exile* (New York: Harcourt Brace, 1994), p. 148. On the significance of exile in Ulmer, see also my 'Perennial Detour: The Cinema of Edgar G. Ulmer and the Experience of Exile', *Cinema Journal*, vol. 43 no. 2 (Winter 2004), pp. 3–25.
60 For a more thorough analysis, see Flinn, *Strains of Utopia*, pp. 124–6. See also Tag Gallagher's instructive discussion in 'All Lost in Wonder: Edgar G. Ulmer', in the Australian online journal *Screening the Past* (March 2001), <www.latrobe.edu.au/screeningthepast/firstrelease/fr0301/tgafr12a.htm>, accessed 3 March 2003.
61 Paul A. Cantor, 'Film Noir and the Frankfurt School: America as Wasteland in Edgar Ulmer's *Detour*', in Mark T. Conrad (ed.), *Philosophy and Film Noir* (Lexington, KY: University Press of Kentucky, 2006), pp. 149–50. Caryl Flinn offers additional weight to the argument: 'To both Al and Adorno, jazz functions as the art of a decaying culture, a music that fails to deliver the unifying comforts of classical works.' See her *Strains of Utopia*, p. 125.

62 The term 'sarcastic disfiguration' comes from Ulman, 'Edgar G. Ulmer'.
63 Bill Krohn, 'King of the Bs', *Film Comment*, vol. 19 no. 4 (July–August 1983), p. 60. Krohn notes later in his insightful essay that Ulmer's foray into ethnic pictures, in particular the four Yiddish films he directed in the late 30s, 'permitted him to explore his own condition of exile and his mixed feelings about being the inheritor of an alien tradition' (p. 64).
64 Anthony Heilbut, *Exiled in Paradise: German Refugee Artists and Intellectuals in America from the 1930s to the Present* (Berkeley: University of California Press, 1997), p. 27.
65 Edward Dimendberg, 'Down these Seen Streets a Man Must Go: Siegfried Kracauer, "Hollywood's Terror Films", and the Spatiality of Film Noir', *New German Critique*, no. 89 (Spring/Summer 2003), p. 138.
66 On the theme of homelessness in Ulmer, see my 'Permanent Vacation: Home and Homelessness in the Life and Work of Edgar G. Ulmer', in Sabine Eckmann and Lutz Koepnick (eds), *Caught by Politics: Hitler Exiles and American Visual Culture in the 1930s and 1940s* (New York: Palgrave, 2007), pp. 175–94.
67 Grissemann, *Mann im Schatten*, p. 222. Andrew Britton also pursues this line of inquiry in his analysis: 'None of the central characters in *Detour* has a fixed abode, and the marginal figures with a settled existence and a role to play in the maintenance and reproduction of what remains of social life are engaged in occupations – running motels and

diners, policing highways, buying and selling cars – which relate in some way to the wandering of others.

Ulmer emphasizes the protagonists' social rootlessness through their propensity to change their identities. Al becomes Haskell, Vera becomes the new Haskell's wife, and Haskell himself has written a letter to his father in which he pretends to be a salesman of hymnals' (p. 182).

68 Thomas Elsaesser, *Weimar Cinema and After: Germany's Historical Imaginary* (New York: Routledge, 2000), p. 374.
69 Cited in Polito, 'Some Detours to *Detour*', p. 145.
70 Grissemann, *Mann im Schatten*, p. 219.
71 Polito, 'Some Detours to *Detour*', p. 158.
72 Grissemann, *Mann im Schatten*, p. 219.
73 Cited in Polito, 'Some Detours to *Detour*', p. 158. It is Eddie Muller who dubs *Two-Man Submarine* 'a waterlogged wartime adventure'. See *Dark City Dames*, p. 153.
74 See Paul Schrader, 'Notes on Film Noir', *Film Comment*, vol. 8 no. 1 (Spring 1972), reprinted in John Belton (ed.), *Movies and Mass Culture* (New Brunswick, NJ: Rutgers University Press, 1996), pp. 153–70. See also Naremore, *More than Night*.
75 Belton, 'Film Noir's Knights of the Road', p. 7.
76 Hossein Amini, 'Hearts of Darkness', *Sight & Sound*, vol. 6 no. 10 (October 1996), p. 61.
77 Cited in A. G., 'Auteur Detour', an appendix to Goldsmith's script reprinted in *Scenario*, p. 180. Goldsmith adds to this: 'We had seven days to shoot the damn thing. This wasn't just a cheap movie, this was the cheapest movie ever made! That's what I'm most proud of' (p. 181).
78 Richard Combs, 'Detour', *Monthly Film Bulletin*, vol. 49 no. 582 (July 1982), p. 146.
79 See Thom Andersen, 'Red Hollywood', in Suzanne Ferguson and Barbara Groseclose (eds), *Literature and the Visual Arts in Contemporary Society* (Columbus: Ohio State University Press, 1985), pp. 141–96, here pp. 183 and 187. I am also indebted to James Naremore's discussion in *More than Night*, pp. 123–35, and to Joshua Hirsch, 'Film Gris Reconsidered', *The Journal of Popular Film and Television*, vol. 34 no. 2 (2006), pp. 82–93.
80 Dana Polan, 'Detour', *Senses of Cinema* (July 2002), <www.sensesofcinema.com/contents/cteq/02/21/detour.html>, accessed 1 August 2003. More impressionistically, Vincent Canby has observed of *Detour*, 'Although this is quintessential *film noir*, the landscapes are mostly shades of pale grey.' See his 'A Forgotten Voice from the Fatalistic World of Film Noir', *The New York Times*, 3 July 1992.
81 Andersen, 'Red Hollywood', p. 187.
82 As Paul Cantor asserts, 'The truck driver looking for companionship who approaches Roberts at the beginning of the film stands for all Americans.' See Cantor, 'Film Noir and the Frankfurt School', p. 155.
83 George Lipsitz, *Time Passages: Collective Memory and American Popular Culture* (Minneapolis: University of Minnesota Press, 1990), p. 201.

84 Chinen Biesen, *Blackout*, pp. 163–4.
85 In his discussion of wartime
productions, Andrew Spicer highlights
Detour as a key example of the
'oppositional mode of film-making
which challenged mainstream
practices'. See his *Film Noir* (London:
Longman, 2002), p. 31.
James Naremore makes mention of
Jacques Rivette's phrase in *More than
Night*, p. 137.
86 Naremore, *More than Night*, p. 149.
87 Britton, 'Detour', p. 183.
88 Donald Lyons, 'Detours', *Film
Comment*, vol. 27 no. 4 (July–August
1991), pp. 2–3. As James Naremore puts
it, 'Like a great many films noirs about
the open road, *Detour* represents the
western frontier as a desert and the
quest for individual freedom as a
meaningless circle or a trap.' See his
More than Night, p. 148. See also film-
maker Walter Salles's 'Notes for a
Theory of the Road Movie', *New York
Times Magazine* (11 November 2007), in
which he suggests that, as a road movie,
Detour gives 'an account of a country
plagued by individualism and greed'.
89 Michael Henry Wilson, 'Edgar G.
Ulmer: "Let there be Light!"', in *Divini
Apparizioni: Edgar G. Ulmer, Joseph Losey,
Leonid Trauberg* (Milan: Transeuropa,
1999), p. 253.
90 Dana Polan, 'California through the
Lens of Hollywood', in Stephanie Barron
et al. (eds), *Reading California: Art, Image,
and Identity, 1900–2000* (Berkeley:
University of California Press, 2000),
pp. 137–9. See also Jonathan F. Bell's
discussion of *Detour* in his 'Shadows in
the Hinterland: Rural Noir', in Mark

Lamster (ed.), *Architecture and Film* (New
York: Princeton Architectural Press,
2000), p. 224.
91 Theodor Adorno, *Minima Moralia:
Reflections from Damaged Life*, trans.
E. F. N. Jephcott (London: Verso, 1978),
p. 48.
92 Polan, 'California through the Lens
of Hollywood', p. 139.
93 Cited in the revised and expanded
German version of Bogdanovich's
interview in *Filmhefte*, no. 1 (Summer
1975), p. 36.
94 I am indebted to James Naremore's
discussion in *More than Night*, pp. 147–8.
95 Unpublished letter of 1 July 1941,
Edgar G. Ulmer to Shirley Ulmer, The
Edgar G. Ulmer Collection, Margaret
Herrick Library.
96 Cited in Williams, 'Edgar Ulmer's
Dark Excursion', p. 25.
97 Lyons, *Death on the Cheap*, p. 10.
98 Polan, 'Detour'.
99 Grissemann, *Mann im Schatten*, p. 227.
100 Foster Hirsch, *Detours and Lost
Highways: A Map of Neo-Noir* (New York:
Limelight Editions, 1999), p. 23.
101 Howard Thompson, 'The Cavern
Bows on Local Screens', *The New York
Times*, 25 December 1965.
102 Edgar G. Ulmer, 'The Loser'
(alternatively 'The Loner'), was
registered with the Screen Writers Guild
West in 1969. The typescript bears a
handwritten note that it was re-
registered in 1983, over ten years after
Ulmer's death; it also has the
handwritten parenthetical '(Detour)'
added to the given title of 'The Loser', as
it is listed on the 'Cast of Characters'
page and the first page of the 111-page

script. All references to 'The Loser' come from the typescript contained in the The Edgar G. Ulmer Collection, Margaret Herrick Library.

103 In the two synopses of *Detour* submitted to the Production Code Administration, after Joseph I. Breen's memo of 1 November 1944 was received by Martin Mooney, Sue at the close of the film marries a big-shot gambler Tony Dillon – in one case (dated 29 December 1944) this takes place right after Al is picked up by the cops, in the second case (undated) just before, with Al stumbling by the chapel in which the ceremony takes place. Ulmer seems to have spared Al that additional agony; or perhaps he simply didn't have the extra film stock to shoot it. See the PCA files on *Detour* at the Margaret Herrick Library.

104 Unpublished letter of 1 July 1941, Edgar G. Ulmer to Shirley Ulmer, The Edgar G. Ulmer Collection, Margaret Herrick Library. In the same letter, Ulmer announces his plans to do a remake of *The Blue Angel* starring Veronica Lake.

105 Peter Bart, 'How to be a Loner in Hollywood', *The New York Times*, 13 March 1966.

106 See David Houston, 'The Two Tom Neals: A Legacy', *Filmfax*, no. 11 (July 1988), p. 27.

107 Arthur Lyons, 'Killer Career – Actor Tom Neal', *Palm Springs Life* (August 1999), <www.palmspringslife.com/>, accessed 18 June 2007. See also the accounts in Muller, *Dark City*, p. 179; and in Marcus, *The Shape of Things to Come*, p. 137.

108 Atkinson, 'Noir and Away', p. 34. As he puts it earlier in the same essay, 'Wade Williams's *Detour* is an ostensible remake of the Ulmer film that plays more like a druggy reincarnation of the first film, brought back to shambling life for the sheer retro love of it.'

109 David Thomson, *The New Biographical Dictionary of Film* (New York: Knopf, 2002), p. 888.

110 The debate over proper credit being given to Goldsmith as the true creator of *Detour* continued to stir as late as summer 1999, when Goldsmith's wife Estela published an impassioned letter in the *Los Angeles Times* (15 August 1999), claiming that 'the writer in Hollywood is continually being short-changed as the creative source of many a movie'.

111 Hirsch, *Detours and Lost Highways*, p. 23.

112 Bert Rebhandl, 'Lauter Umwege zum Ruhm', *Frankfurter Allgemeine Zeitung*, 10 April 2003. Vincent Canby puts a more positive spin on things in his review: 'For reasons not easily explained, the existence of a "Detour" remake seems absolutely in keeping with the whole film noir ethos – sad, hustling and sinfully entertaining.' See Canby, 'A Forgotten Voice'.

113 Marcus, *The Shape of Things to Come*, pp. 130–1.

114 Ibid., p. 136.

115 Myron Meisel calls *Detour* 'an exercise in sustained perversity' (Meisel, 'The Primacy of the Visual', p. 150); the notion of an Ulmer film like

Detour 'dripping with disgust' comes from Thomson, *New Biographical Dictionary of Film*, p. 888.
116 Lizzie Francke, 'My Festival', *Scotland on Sunday*, 10 August 1997.
117 John Ashbery, '*Detour* (IV)', *LIT*, no. 13 (Autumn 2007), p. 138. In a contemporary musical register, Brazilian-born DJ Amon Tobin recently remixed his version of *Detour* against a lush score of ambient sounds and break beats and posted it on *YouTube*: <www.youtube.com/watch?v=xmEw6AgURwY>.

Credits

Detour
USA/1945

Directed by
Edgar G. Ulmer
Produced by
Leon Fromkess
Screenplay and Original Story
Martin Goldsmith
Director of Photography
Benjamin H. Kline
Edited by
George McGuire
Art Director
Edward C. Jewell
Musical Score
Erdody
[i.e. Leo Erdody]

©PRC Pictures, Inc.
Production Company
A PRC production

Associate Producer
Martin Mooney
Production Manager
Raoul Pagel
Assistant Director
William A. Calihan, Jr

Dialogue Director
Ben Coleman
Set Decorator
Glenn P. Thompson
Wardrobe Designer
Mona Barry
Director of Make-up
Bud Westmore
Sound Engineer
Max Hutchinson
Sound System
Western Electric

CAST
Tom Neal
Al Roberts
Ann Savage
Vera
Claudia Drake
Sue Harvey
Edmund MacDonald
Charles Haskell, Jr
Tim Ryan
Gus, diner proprietor
Esther Howard
Hedy, waitress
Pat Gleason
Joe, truck driver

uncredited
Roger Clark
Dillon, a cop
Don Brodie
used-car salesman
Eddie Hall
used-car mechanic
Harry Strang
California border patrolman

Filmed from 25–30 June 1945 (35mm, black and white, mono)

US theatrical release by Producers Releasing Corporation on 30 November 1945. Running time: 67 minutes
UK theatrical release by Pathe Pictures Ltd, c. October 1946. Running time: 68 minutes 3 seconds, BBFC certificate A

Credits compiled by Julian Grainger

Bibliography

Amini, Hossein, 'Hearts of Darkness', *Sight & Sound*, vol. 6 no. 10 (October 1996), p. 61.

Andersen, Thom, 'Red Hollywood', in Suzanne Ferguson and Barbara Groseclose (eds), *Literature and the Visual Arts in Contemporary Society* (Columbus: Ohio State University Press, 1985), pp. 141–96.

Atkinson, Michael, 'Noir and Away', *Bright Lights*, no. 15 (Winter 1995), pp. 30–5.

Belton, John, 'Edgar G. Ulmer', in Jean-Pierre Coursodon (ed.), *American Directors*, vol. 1 (New York: McGraw-Hill, 1983), pp. 339–47.

——, *Howard Hawks, Frank Borzage, Edgar G. Ulmer* (New York: A. S. Barnes & Co., 1974).

Biesen, Sheri Chinen, *Blackout: World War II and the Origins of Film Noir* (Baltimore: Johns Hopkins University Press, 2005).

Bogdanovich, Peter, 'Edgar G. Ulmer', *Who the Devil Made It: Conversations with Legendary Film Directors* (New York: Ballantine, 1998), pp. 558–604.

Britton, Andrew, 'Detour', in Ian Cameron (ed.), *The Book of Film Noir* (New York: Continuum, 1993), pp. 174–83.

Cantor, Paul A., 'Film Noir and the Frankfurt School: America as Wasteland in Edgar Ulmer's *Detour*', in Mark T. Conrad (ed.), *Philosophy and Film Noir* (Lexington, KY: University Press of Kentucky, 2006), pp. 139–61.

Cargnelli, Christian and Michael Omasta (eds), *Schatten. Exil: Europäische Emigranten im Film Noir* (Vienna: PVS, 1997).

Combs, Richard, 'Detour', *Monthly Film Bulletin*, vol. 49 no. 582 (July 1982), pp. 145–6.

Coursen, David, 'Closing Down the Open Road: Detour', *Movietone News*, no. 48 (February 1978), pp. 16–19.

'Detour: A Symposium on Edgar Ulmer's 1945 PRC Film Noir', *LIT*, no. 13 (Autumn 2007), pp. 130–61.

Dixon, Wheeler (ed.), *Producers Releasing Corporation: A Comprehensive Filmography and History* (Jefferson, NC: McFarland, 1986).

Elsaesser, Thomas, *Weimar Cinema and After: Germany's Historical Imaginary* (New York: Routledge, 2000).

Flynn, Charles and Todd McCarthy (eds), *Kings of the Bs: Working within the Hollywood System* (New York: E. P. Dutton & Co., 1975).

Gallagher, Tag, 'All Lost in Wonder: Edgar G. Ulmer', *Screening the Past* (March 2001), <www.latrobe.edu.au/ screeningthepast/firstrelease/fr0301/ tgafr12a.htm>.

Goldsmith, Martin, *Detour: An Extraordinary Tale* (New York: Macaulay, 1939).

——, 'Detour', *Scenario*, vol. 3 no. 2 (Summer 1997), pp. 133–78.

Grissemann, Stefan, *Mann im Schatten: Der Filmemacher Edgar G. Ulmer* (Vienna: Zsolnay, 2003).

Heilbut, Anthony, *Exiled in Paradise: German Refugee Artists and Intellectuals in America from the 1930s to the Present* (Berkeley:

University of California Press, 1997).

Hirsch, Foster, *Detours and Lost Highways: A Map of Neo-Noir* (New York: Limelight Editions, 1999).

Isenberg, Noah, 'Perennial Detour: The Cinema of Edgar G. Ulmer and the Experience of Exile', *Cinema Journal*, vol. 43 no. 2 (Winter 2004), pp. 3–25.

——, 'Permanent Vacation: Home and Homelessness in the Life and Work of Edgar G. Ulmer', in Sabine Eckmann and Lutz Koepnick (eds), *Caught by Politics: Hitler Exiles and American Visual Culture in the 1930s and 1940s* (New York: Palgrave, 2007), pp. 175–94.

Krohn, Bill, 'King of the Bs', *Film Comment*, vol. 19 no. 4 (July–August 1983), pp. 60–4.

Lyons, Arthur, *Death on the Cheap: The Lost B Movies of Film Noir* (New York: Da Capo, 2000).

Lyons, Donald, 'Detours', *Film Comment*, vol. 27 no. 4 (July–August 1991), pp. 2–3.

Marcus, Greil, *The Shape of Things to Come: Prophecy and the American Voice* (New York: Farrar, Straus and Giroux, 2006).

Modleski, Tania, 'Film Theory's Detour', *Screen*, vol. 23 no. 5 (November–December 1982), pp. 72–9.

Moullet, Luc, 'Présentation Edgar G. Ulmer', *Cahiers du cinéma*, no. 58 (April 1956), pp. 55–7.

Muller, Eddie, *Dark City: The Lost World of Film Noir* (New York: St Martin's Griffin, 1998).

——, *Dark City Dames: The Wicked Women of Film Noir* (New York: HarperCollins, 2001).

Naremore, James, *More than Night: Film Noir and its Contexts* (Berkeley: University of California Press, 1998).

Nau, Peter, 'Das Geheimnis der Form in den Filmen Edgar G. Ulmers', in Christian Cargnelli and Michael Omasta (eds), *Aufbruch ins Ungewisse: Österreichische Filmschaffende in der Emigration vor 1945* (Vienna: Wespennest, 1993), pp.117–31.

Polan, Dana, 'California through the Lens of Hollywood', in Stephanie Barron *et al.* (eds), *Reading California: Art, Image, and Identity, 1900–2000* (Berkeley: University of California Press, 2000), pp. 128–50.

——, 'Detour', *Senses of Cinema* (July 2002), <www.sensesofcinema. com/contents/cteq/02/21/detour. html>.

Tesson, Charles, 'Hollywood ou mourir', *Cahiers du cinéma*, no. 436 (October 1990), pp. 50–4.

Ulman, Erik, 'Edgar G. Ulmer', *Senses of Cinema* (January–February 2003), <www.sensesofcinema.com/ contents/directors/03/ulmer.html>.

Williams, Wade, 'Edgar Ulmer's Dark Excursion into the Nightmare World of Fatal Irony . . .', *Filmfax*, no. 11 (July 1988), pp. 22–5.

Wilson, Michael Henry, 'Edgar G. Ulmer: "Let there be Light!"', in *Divini Apparizioni: Edgar G. Ulmer, Joseph Losey, Leonid Trauberg* (Milan: Transeuropa, 1999), pp. 249–55.